The Rocks Cry Out

The Rocks Cry Out

A Christian Guide to Stones, Gems & Crystals

by Jody Thomae

THE ROCKS CRY OUT: A CHRISTIAN GUIDE TO STONES, GEMS & CRYSTALS

Copyright © 2022 Jody Thomae. Ashland, Ohio. All rights reserved. Except for brief quotations in publications or reviews, this book may not be reproduced without prior written permission from the author. Permission without written consent is granted for up to five (5) pages to be photocopied for personal use if copyright information (at bottom of each page) is legible and visible. Contact yogafaithjody@gmail.com for written consent beyond five pages.

ISBN 9798827532705
Manufactured in the U.S.A.

Bible translations used:

Scripture quotations marked AMP are from The Amplified® Bible © 2015 by The Lockman Foundation. Used by permission. www.Lockman.org.

Scripture quotations marked ESV are from The ESV® Bible (The Holy Bible, English Standard Version®) © 2001 by Crossway, a publishing ministry of Good News Publishers. ESV® Text Edition: 2011.

Scripture quotations marked MSG are from The Message © 1993, 2002, 2018 by Eugene H. Peterson. Used by permission of NavPress Publishing Group.

Scripture quotations marked NIV are from THE HOLY BIBLE, NEW INTERNATIONAL VERSION®, NIV® © 1973, 1978, 1984, 2011 by Biblica, Inc.™ Used by permission. All rights reserved worldwide.

Scripture quotations marked NLT are from Holy Bible, New Living Translation © 1996, 2004, 2015 by Tyndale House Foundation. Used by permission of Tyndale House Publishers Inc., Carol Stream, Illinois. All rights reserved.

Scripture quotations marked TPT are from The Passion Translation®. © 2017, 2018, 2020 by Passion & Fire Ministries, Inc. Used by permission. All rights reserved. ThePassionTranslation.com.

Scripture quotations marked VOICE are from The Voice Bible Copyright © 2012 Thomas Nelson, Inc. The Voice™ translation © 2012 Ecclesia Bible Society. All rights reserved.

To my brothers... thanks for liking rocks too.

Table of Contents

Introduction / 1 - 6

African Turquoise / 7
Agate / 7 - 19
Alabaster / 20
Amazonite / 20
Amber / 21
Amethyst / 21 - 22
Angelite / 23
Aquamarine / 23
Aventurine / 24
Bloodstone / 25
Bronzite / 25
Carnelian / 26
Cat's Eye / 26
Chalcedony / 27
Chrysocolla / 27
Chrysoprase / 28
Citrine / 29
Coral / 29 - 30
Diamond / 30
Emerald / 31
Flourite / 32
Garnet / 32 - 33
Gold Sandstone / 33
Hematite / 33
Howlite / 34
Iolite / 34
Jade / 35 - 36
Jasper / 37 - 49
Kyanite / 49
Labradorite / 49 - 50
Lapis Lazuli / 50
Larimar / 51
Lepidolite / 51

Malachite / 52
Moonstone / 52 - 53
Morganite / 54
Obsidian / 54 - 55
Onyx / 55 - 56
Opal / 56 - 58
Pearl / 58
Pietersite / 59
Prehnite / 59
Pyrite / 60
Quartz / 60 - 65
River Stone / 65
Rhyolite / 66
Ruby / 66
Sapphire / 67
Sardonyx / 67 - 68
Selenite / 68
Serpentine / 69
Sodalite / 69
Sunset Dumortierite / 70
Sunstone / 70
Tiger's Eye / 71
Topaz / 72
Tourmaline / 72 - 73
Turquoise / 73 - 74
Unakite / 74
Wonderstone / 74
Wood Opalite / 75

Praying With Prayer Beads / 76 - 84
Color Meanings / 85 - 86
About the Author / 87
References / 89

*Who is the True God
except the Eternal?
Who stands like a ROCK
except our God?
The True God
who encircled me
with strength
and made
my pathway straight.*

Psalm 18:31-32

Let the Rocks Cry Out

From my childhood, I have loved rocks.

Hiking along the trails of the Mohican Forest, I was surrounded by boulders, caves, rock formations, and a cliff carved from sandstone by the smallest trickle of water, forming a "waterfall" that flowed to the river beyond. On our way back along the trail, we'd scramble along the rocks by the river, my brothers fighting for dominance in a game of King-of-the-Hill on the largest boulder they could find, while I (being the youngest, smallest, and the only girl) would crouch by the river's edge. There, under the surface of the water, stones would glisten and call out to me to pick them up. Shoving them in my pockets, I'd take them home as treasure found in our wild and watery exploration. Of course, once I got them home and pulled them from the recesses of my deep pockets, I would find that now dry, they weren't nearly as lustrous as they had seemed at water's edge.

I also remember digging through the bins of small polished rocks—you know the bins; they have them at many tourists shops—all bright and colorful and shiny—oh, so shiny! I could look and touch, but we seldom bought. I guess my dad, who had picked up thousands of rocks, clearing them from the farm fields where he grew up, didn't quite see their value.

And then my brother got a rock polisher one year and suddenly we had those same shiny rocks. Although that polisher was so small you would spend days polishing only to have just a few small treasures for all your efforts—which of course he made into jewelry for mom. I might still have one pin he made me.

My other brother loved to collect fossil rocks from the creek near our home. When we sold our parent's house, we literally took bag upon bag back to the creek, returning these prehistoric treasures to their rightful owner—the woods, the water, the wild.

When we were building our home by the edges of the lake near Mohican Forest, I jokingly gave myself the auspicious title of "Lead Geologist" as I sifted through piles of dirt and found rocks and minerals of all sorts, shapes, and sizes. We unearthed so many rocks on our property I was determined that we would not pay for a single rock for our future landscaping dreams. I collected piles upon piles—from baseball sized river rocks to large granite boulders that now hold our stone steps that lead down the hill to the lake in place. Some were worn smooth by waterways that have coursed through the land for centuries. Others had somehow escaped the water's erosion—jagged and rough with specks of feldspar reflecting the sunlight.

Not sure exactly why I love rocks so much. Perhaps it's the variety? Perhaps it's the Artist's painstaking attention to detail? God could have made all rocks gray and uniform, but he chose to make them in different types and colors and forms. Like an artist, he spared no color on his palette and painted them with all the colors of the rainbow. Some are opaque, others translucent or clear—their crystallized forms reflecting and refracting the light as it passes through. Even their shapes differ, from the crystal prisms of quartz, to the smooth, round shapes of river stone, to the flaky layers of slate. Each one crying out and declaring the creativity of our God!

When the Pharisees told Jesus to make his disciples stop crying out in worship as he entered Jerusalem on a donkey, he replied, "I tell you, if these [worshipers] were silent, the very stones would cry out" (Luke 19:40). He was possibly referencing a passage in Habakkuk 2:11 that says that the stones in the wall and the rafters in the ceiling will cry out against the injustice of those who have exploited others for their own wealth. Jesus is making use of hyperbole and anthropomorphism—he knows the rocks won't literally cry out. Yet, something in my spirit tells me he knew they've been crying out all along.

Rocks inform us of the creation of this world and the formation of the landscape around us. Striated layers tell of years long ago with many different weather patterns and atmospheric conditions, and heaved up in varied directions, they reveal the shifting of tectonic plates below. Colors brought on by various minerals within speak of the wealth of raw materials in our world. Rocks formed by meteorites and volcanoes are the only survivors to tell the stories of catastrophic events many thousands of years ago. Even staurolite, the Fairy Cross, tells the story of One who would save the world through a final act of love that would require his very life.

Yes, they are certainly crying out.

The earth is the LORD's, and everything in it.
Psalm 24:1 NLT

Because of my love for rocks and the stories they tell, I am also curious about their history, symbolism, and meanings. Rock "meanings" go back to ancient times. Cultures long past gave stones unique meanings and attributed them with special powers. These were often connected to their color, texture, and appearance. Stones were carried or worn as protective talismans and good luck charms. Ancient engravers would carve them into beautiful cameos and intaglios (many of those are still in existence today). Stones, gems, and minerals were carried and traded along prehistoric trade routes dating back to the second millennium BC. In fact, the trading of amber by Baltic travelers goes back almost 10,000 years! As these stones made their away across continents and cultures, the beliefs about their symbolism traveled with them. Traders told the tales of their powers and cosmic origins.

Scripturally, there are over 1,700 references to gemstones and minerals in the Bible—with 124 Greek and Hebrew words referring to them. You'll see their symbolism often reflected in the passages that mention them. However, it is important to note that gem identification was hardly an exact science (or a science of any kind) in ancient times. Gems were mostly identified by color and not internal structure or mineral composition. So, for example, green gems of any kind were all called by the same name, regardless of whether they were an emerald, jade, or malachite. Moreover, the precise meaning of the words used to describe the gems was lost over time, and translators (who were not gemologists or mineralogists) did their best guesswork at identifying what gems were being referred to in various passages. Generally they used what they were familiar with to fill in the blanks when necessary. So we must keep that in mind when we read passages that mention gems and minerals. It also explains why Bible translations used a variety of names in the same passages.

There are three passages that stand out in terms of gems and minerals: Exodus 28 (The Breastplate of Aaron); Ezekiel 28:12b-17 (The Fall of Satan); and Revelation 21:18-23 (The New Jerusalem). Take them in now....

> *Fashion a breastpiece for making decisions—the work of skilled hands. Make it like the ephod: of gold, and of blue, purple and scarlet yarn, and of finely twisted linen. It is to be square—a span long and a span wide—and folded double. Then mount four rows of precious stones on it. The first row shall be carnelian, chrysolite and beryl; the second row shall be turquoise, lapis lazuli and emerald; the third row shall be jacinth, agate and amethyst; the fourth row shall be topaz, onyx and jasper. Mount them in gold filigree settings. There are to be twelve stones, one for each of the names of the sons of Israel, each engraved like a seal with the name of one of the twelve tribes. Exodus 28:15-21 NIV*

*You were the seal of perfection,
full of wisdom and perfect in beauty.
You were in Eden, the garden of God;
every precious stone adorned you:
carnelian, chrysolite and emerald, topaz,
onyx and jasper, lapis lazuli, turquoise and beryl.
Your settings and mountings were made of gold;
on the day you were created they were prepared.
You were anointed as a guardian cherub, for so I ordained you.
You were on the holy mount of God;
you walked among the fiery stones.
You were blameless in your ways from the day you were created
till wickedness was found in you.
Through your widespread trade
you were filled with violence, and you sinned.
So I drove you in disgrace from the mount of God,
and I expelled you, guardian cherub, from among the fiery stones.
Your heart became proud on account of your beauty,
and you corrupted your wisdom because of your splendor.
So I threw you to the earth... Ezekiel 28:12b-17 NIV*

The wall was built of jasper, while the city was pure gold, like clear glass. The foundations of the wall of the city were adorned with every kind of jewel. The first was jasper, the second sapphire, the third agate, the fourth emerald, the fifth onyx, the sixth carnelian, the seventh chrysolite, the eighth beryl, the ninth topaz, the tenth chrysoprase, the eleventh jacinth, the twelfth amethyst. And the twelve gates were twelve pearls, each of the gates made of a single pearl, and the street of the city was pure gold, like transparent glass. And I saw no temple in the city, for its temple is the Lord God the Almighty and the Lamb. And the city has no need of sun or moon to shine on it, for the glory of God gives it light, and its lamp is the Lamb. Revelation 21:18-23 ESV

From theses passages, you can see the great value given to these stones. They were considered precious items of beauty—worthy to cry out praises to their Creator and render justice where the balance had been tipped towards evil.

In the following pages you will find a listing of stones. It is not exhaustive or definitive—it is not a rock-identifying encyclopedia with pictures[1] (see recommendations in footnotes). My purpose is to offer an inexpensive, general resource for Christian jewelry designers, gem collectors, and "rock heads" like me to find Biblical meaning in stones.

In my own search for stone meanings, I have struggled to find a list that wasn't based in New Age philosophy or pagan belief systems. I've spent several years gleaning and adapting symbolic meanings from the tales, legends, and lore that surround these rocks—in some cases I'll share the lore and legends. In other cases, the meaning and symbolism, like the ancients, is based on its color, texture, and attributes. You will notice I use the phrase "said to" or "believed to"—please note that these are references to the lore that surrounds them. Each stone entry includes Bible verses to accompany and enhance its symbolism and meaning. I've also included ideas for praying with prayer beads and a list of color meanings from scripture as two other helpful resources at the end of the book.

I pray these gleanings enhance your rock climbing and collecting, your bead stringing and jewelry making, and perhaps... your ability to pick the perfect gem for the one you love!

And remember: ultimately it boils down to the words of my friend Michelle Thielen:

"We do not worship the stones; we worship the Stonemaker!"

Hallelujah! May we always join in creation, crying out in worship, wonder, and awe at the beauty of our Creator....

For you shall go out in joy and be led forth in peace;
the mountains and the hills before you
shall break forth into singing,
and all the trees of the field shall clap their hands.
Isaiah 55:12 ESV

---

[1] I recommend the app available at rockidentifier.com and a good encyclopedia which will run you about $25 on Amazon.

African Turquoise

African Turquoise is actually a speckled, teal-colored jasper found in Africa. It often contains inclusions such as copper and iron, creating veins and mottling that ranges in color from rust to black. Symbolizes transformation, evolution, and awakening to your highest spiritual purpose.

Jeremiah 29:11-14 NLT: "For I know the plans I have for you," says the Lord. "They are plans for good and not for disaster, to give you a future and a hope. In those days when you pray, I will listen. If you look for me wholeheartedly, you will find me. I will be found by you," says the Lord.

Agate

Amulets cut from agate go back to ancient civilization. Most often they were blessed by a priest or shaman and carried for protection. Ancients believed agates would protect one from storms and spiders. I don't know about you, but I need some agates on my screened porch where all the spiders hide! All kidding aside, agates are a beautiful stone with layers and inclusions that make them extremely interesting to examine up close. They have long been admired for their incredible beauty.

Agate has a dreamy quality with signature bands created by mineral deposits layered in a wavelike circular pattern around its circumference. Classified as a chalcedony, they are a fine-grained variety of the quartz family and come in vast array of colors and "designs"—each one a work of art!

Known as "The Stabilizer," it symbolizes support, centering, and grounding. Along with its supportive energy, agates are said to bring emotional, physical, and mental balance. Agate has a lower intensity and vibrates at a slower frequency than other stones, so agate works slowly but brings great strength. Said to cleanse, eliminate, and transform negativity. With their soothing and calming energy, they are said to heal inner anger or tension and create a sense of security and safety.

Isaiah 33:6 TPT: He will be your constant source of stability in changing times, and out of his abundant love he gives you the riches of salvation, wisdom, and knowledge.
Yes, the fear of the Lord is the key to this treasure!

Isaiah 33:6 MSG: God is supremely esteemed. His center holds. Zion brims over with all that is just and right.
God keeps your days stable and secure — salvation, wisdom, and knowledge in surplus, and best of all, Zion's treasure, Fear-of-God.

Varieties of Agates:

Australian Agate—said to eliminate and transform negativity, and enhance mental function by improving concentration, perception, and analytical abilities. Australian agate dates back over three billion years!

Psalm 102:25-28 TPT: With your hands you once formed the foundations of the earth and handcrafted the heavens above.
They will all fade away one day like worn-out clothing, ready to be discarded, but you'll still be here.
You will replace it all! Your first creation will be changed, but you alone will endure, the God of all eternity!
Generation after generation our descendants will live securely, for you are the one protecting us, keeping us for yourself.

Black Agate—symbolizes protection from danger and power against forces of darkness, and is said to bring emotions into equilibrium. Black agate represents courage, energy, strength, fighting fear, and self-confidence.

Psalm 56:3-4 AMP: When I am afraid,
I will put my trust *and* faith in You.
In God, whose word I praise;
In God I have put my trust;
I shall not fear.
What can mere man do to me?

Blue Crab Fire Agate—symbolizes creativity, individuality, courage, inspiration, encouragement, healing, restoration.

Romans 12:1 TPT: Beloved friends, what should be our proper response to God's marvelous mercies? I encourage you to surrender yourselves to God to be his sacred, living sacrifices. And live in holiness, experiencing all that delights his heart. For this becomes your genuine expression of worship.

Blue Lace Agate—a stone of communication, it is said to help those who have difficulty being heard by others or who need confidence and articulation to share their truths. Symbolizes clarity of thought and unwavering intent in regards to what matters most.

> Isaiah 12:3-4 MSG: Joyfully you'll pull up buckets of water from the wells of salvation. And as you do it, you'll say, "Give thanks to God. Call out his name. Ask him anything! Shout to the nations, tell them what he's done, spread the news of his great reputation!"

Blue Sky Agate—symbolizes calmness and harmony. Blue sky agate has been known through time as a talisman with great healing energies. It is said that it lessens negative energies and stress, endowing us with a sense of peace and tranquility. Also said to assist with verbal expression of thoughts and feelings.

2 Corinthians 7:5-7 AMP: When we arrived in Macedonia province, we couldn't settle down. The fights in the church and the fears in our hearts kept us on pins and needles. We couldn't relax because we didn't know how it would turn out. Then the God who lifts up the downcast lifted our heads and our hearts with the arrival of [our friend]. We were glad just to see him, but the true reassurance came in what he told us about you: how much you cared, how much you grieved, how concerned you were for me. I went from worry to tranquility in no time!

Botswana Agate — said to have an anti-depressant quality and stimulates the exploration of buried trauma and wounding. Symbolizes the mining of buried treasure in our soul.

Isaiah 45:2-7 MSG: I'll go ahead of you, clearing and paving the road. I'll break down bronze city gates, smash padlocks, kick down barred entrances. I'll lead you to buried treasures, secret caches of valuables — confirmations that it is in fact, I, God, the God of Israel, who calls you by name. It's because of my dear servant Jacob, Israel my chosen, that I've singled you out, called you by name, and given you this privileged work. And you don't even know me! I am God, the only God there is. Besides me there are no real gods. I'm the one who armed you for this work, though you don't even know me, so that everyone, from east to west, will know that I have no rival. I am God, the only God there is. I form light and create darkness; I make harmonies and create discords. I, God, do all these things.

Cherry Blossom Sakura Agate — the stone of dreamers and over-comers, symbolizes "reblooming" after painful or exhausting periods in life. It is said to help you nurture and manifest your dreams, but without striving and making them happen on your own. A perfect stone to wear when launching a new venture, as it is thought to add weight to your endeavor and help you reach your goals. Cherry Blossom agate has a kind of soft feminine energy that fires up the passion and pursuit for dreams in the wearers. It encourages people to live life the way they want, to the fullest.

Revelation 3:7-12 NLT: These are the words of the One who is holy and true, who holds the key of David. What he opens no one can shut, and what he shuts no one can open. I know your deeds. See, I have placed before you an open door that no one can shut. I know that you have little strength, yet you have kept my word and have not denied my name. I will make those who are of the synagogue of Satan — I will make them come and fall down at your feet and acknowledge that

I have loved you. Since you have kept my command to endure patiently, I will also keep you from the hour of trial that is going to come on the whole world to test the inhabitants of the earth. I am coming soon. Hold on to what you have, so that no one will take your crown. The one who is victorious I will make a pillar in the temple of my God. Never again will they leave it. I will write on them the name of my God and the name of the city of my God, the new Jerusalem, which is coming down out of heaven from my God; and I will also write on them my new name.

Crazy Lace Agate—called the "Laughter Stone" or "Happy Lace," it is associated with sunny days and dancing, bringing joy to those who wear it. Symbolizes support, encouragement, elevated thoughts, and optimism.

Psalm 126:2-3 NLT: We were filled with laughter, and we sang for joy. And the other nations said, "What amazing things the Lord has done for them." Yes, the Lord has done amazing things for us! What joy!

Cream Agate—a dreamy stone of milky cream, it symbolizes rebalancing and harmonizing of the body, mind and spirit. Said to enhanced mental function, improving concentration, perception, and analytical abilities.

Ephesians 4:29-32 NLT: Don't use foul or abusive language. Let everything you say be good and helpful, so that your words will be an encouragement to those who hear them. And do not bring sorrow to God's Holy Spirit by the way you live. Remember, he has identified you as his own, guaranteeing that you will be saved on the day of redemption. Get rid of all bitterness, rage, anger, harsh words, and slander, as well as all types of evil behavior. Instead, be kind to each other, tenderhearted, forgiving one another, just as God through Christ has forgiven you.

Dendritic Fossil Ocean Agate — known as the "Stone of Plentitude," it is believed to bring abundance and fullness to all areas of life. It has branch-like inclusions of iron or manganese within the colorless to milky white stone.

John 10:7-10 VOICE: I tell you the truth: I am the gate of the sheep. All who approached the sheep before Me came as thieves and robbers, and the sheep did not listen to their voices. I am the gate; whoever enters through Me will be liberated, will go in and go out, and will find pastures. The thief approaches with malicious intent, looking to steal, slaughter, and destroy; I came to give life with joy and abundance.

Dragon Vein Agate — it is thought to prevent the holding back of emotions (think of a dragon "holding back" — not possible!). It is said to help you grab the happiness that you really want.

1 Peter 3:8-9 AMP: Finally, all of you be like-minded [united in spirit], sympathetic, brotherly, kindhearted [courteous and compassionate toward each other as members of one household], and humble in spirit; and never return evil for evil or insult for insult [avoid scolding, berating, and any kind of abuse], but on the contrary, give a blessing [pray for one another's well-being, contentment, and protection]; for you have been called for this very purpose, that you might inherit a blessing [from God that brings well-being, happiness, and protection].

Fire Agate — said to be grounding, centering, stabilizing, and balancing. It is symbolic of that which rises again from the ashes.

I Samuel 2:8-9 NIV: He raises the poor from the dust and lifts the needy from the ash heap; he seats them with princes and has them inherit a throne of honor. For the foundations of the earth are the Lord's; on them he has set the world. He will guard the feet of his faithful servants, but the wicked will be silenced in the place of darkness.

Golden Aqua or Aqua Aura Quartz—thought to calm the emotions and be a powerful stress reliever, reducing or eliminating anger and helping to process emotional disturbances, grief, and traumas to a point that they are no longer stressful. Symbolizes the ability to speak the truth in a calm and loving manner.

Ephesians 4:14-15 TPT: And we will not be easily shaken by trouble, nor led astray by novel teachings or by the false doctrines of deceivers who teach clever lies. But instead we will remain strong and always sincere in our love as we express the truth. All our direction and ministries will flow from Christ and lead us deeper into him, the anointed Head of his body, the church.

Golden Sage Agate—forms in volcanic ash, and features dark manganese dendrites throughout which give some stones the look of moss growing in them. The stone can also include its namesake sage green, cream colors and whites.

> Psalm 119:100-104 TPT: You have graced me with more insight than the old sages because I have not failed to walk in the light of your ways. I refused to bend my morals when temptation was before me so that I could become obedient to your word. I refuse to turn away from difficult truths, for you yourself have taught me to love your words.
> How sweet are your living promises to me;
> sweeter than honey is your revelation-light.
> For your truth is the source of my understanding.

Gray Agate—has a very calm, gentle and steadying presence, encouraging one to be more conscious of their thoughts and feelings and their effect on their long-term well-being. Represents the One who holds the universe in balance.

Isaiah 40:12 NIV: Who has measured the waters in the hollow of his hand, or with the breadth of his hand marked off the heavens? Who has held the dust of the earth in a basket, or weighed the mountains on the scales and the hills in a balance?

Green Terra Agate—contains the best of nature in a variety of small shapes and designs. Symbolizes spiritual healing, growth, soothing support, and stability, encouraging quiet introspection and contemplation.

Psalm 86:10-13 TPT: You are the one and only God. What miracles! What wonders! What greatness belongs to you! Teach me more about you, how you work and how you move, so that I can walk onward in your truth until everything within me brings honor to your name. With all my heart and passion I will thank you, my God! I will give glory to your name, always and forever! You love me so much and you placed your greatness upon me. You rescued me from the deepest place of darkness, and you have delivered me from a certain death.

Indian Agate—known in some cultures as the "Stone of Eternity," it is symbolic of powerful healing. It represents physical strength, emotional security and protection. Said to increase serenity and patience; decrease stress; carry peace and tranquility; and stimulate concentration.

It has mixed colors, but is predominantly green. Green minerals are said to have a harmonizing and neutralizing effect and increase interest and enthusiasm. Green symbolizes initiative, the will to live, abundance, blessing, and success. Green is also the color of hope and renewal.

Song of Songs 2:13 TPT: Can you not discern this new day of destiny breaking forth around you? The early signs of my purposes and plans are bursting forth. The budding vines of new life are now blooming everywhere. The fragrance of their flowers whisper, "There is change in the air." Arise, my love, my beautiful companion, and run with me to the higher place. For now is the time to arise and come away with me.

Lightening Agate—thought to stimulate analytical capabilities and precision, provide perceptiveness, and awaken inherent talents. Also thought to help improve sight and quench thirst. Like lightening blots across the sky, it brings energy and power—just like the Living Water of Jesus!

> Psalm 36:9 VOICE: You have the fountain of life that quenches our thirst. Your light has opened our eyes and awakened our souls.

Madagascar Orange Dendritic Agate—gets its name from a Greek word meaning tree-like and is known as the "Stone of Plentitude"—bringing abundance and fullness to all areas of life. Dendritic agate encourages perseverance and patience, promotes a peaceful inner and outer environment, deepens our own connection to the earth, promotes inner stability, composure, and maturity, and its warm, protective properties encourage security and self-confidence.

Joshua 1:9 VOICE: This is My command: "Be strong and courageous. Never be afraid or discouraged because I am your God, the Eternal One, and I will remain with you wherever you go."

Marine Agate—symbolizes abundance and fullness of life, stabilizing, strengthening, and promoting perseverance, patience, and hope.

Isaiah 35:1-3 NLT: Even the wilderness and desert will be glad in those days. The wasteland will rejoice and blossom with spring crocuses. Yes, there will be an abundance of flowers and singing and joy! The deserts will become as green as the mountains of Lebanon, as lovely as Mount Carmel or the plain of Sharon. There the Lord will display his glory, the splendor of our God. With this news, strengthen those who have tired hands, and encourage those who feel defeated.

Montana Moss Agate—considered the most powerful of the agates and a stone for warriors. This type of moss agate (see next entry) is mined specifically in Montana. A place of adventure, Montana is known as "The Last Frontier" state and "Big Sky" country with its wide-open spaces, towering mountain ranges, and a sky that really is bigger than you can imagine! The early Americans that settled in Montana were mighty courageous people.

Judges 6:12 NIV: When the angel of the Lord appeared to Gideon, he said, "The Lord is with you, mighty warrior." (Note: In this passage, Gideon was hiding from his enemies, the Midianites. The Israelites were surrounded by the Midianites and lived in bondage to their power. When God found Gideon hiding out, God spoke into his potential, not his current state. God wants to do the same for each of us.)

Moss Agate—symbolizes streams of abundance and new beginnings, refreshing the soul and enabling you to see beauty in everything around you. Its hues, colors, and patterns bring you back to nature, no matter how far away you are—it's as if you can breathe in the deep scent of pine, see sunlight through shaded trees, and hear the cooling sound of water running over stone. It's no wonder it's said that moss agate can heal your heart in an instant, help you stay rooted to the world beneath your feet, and keep you feeling cleansed and ready for any changes coming your way.

Psalm 36:7-10 VOICE: Your strong love,
O True God, is precious.
All people run for shelter under the shadow of Your wings.
In Your house, they eat and are full at Your table.
They drink from the river of Your overflowing kindness.
You have the fountain of life that quenches our thirst.
Your light has opened our eyes and awakened our souls.
May Your love continue to grow deeply
in the lives of all who know You.
May Your salvation reach every heart committed to do right.

Phantom Agate—"phantom" crystals are ones that have another crystal within their structure, giving the appearance of a wispy, smoke-like creature within. Symbolizes spiritual healing, growth, soothing support, and stability, encouraging quiet introspection and contemplation within.

>Psalm 27:4-5 AMP:
>One thing I have asked of the Lord,
>and that I will seek:
>That I may dwell in the house of the Lord
>[in His presence] all the days of my life,
>To gaze upon the beauty
>[the delightful loveliness and majestic grandeur]
>of the Lord
>And to meditate in His temple.
>For in the day of trouble
>He will hide me in His shelter;
>In the secret place of His tent
>He will hide me;
>He will lift me up on a rock.

South Red Agate—said to give a vitality to proceed into the future. It is a gemstone to light the fire once again in the heart. Symbolizes the expression of your honest feelings, while at the same time dismissing negative emotional thought patterns that are limiting to your heart and soul.

>Psalm 5:1-3 MSG: Listen, God! Please, pay attention!
>Can you make sense of these ramblings,
>my groans and cries?
>King-God, I need your help.
>Every morning
>you'll hear me at it again.
>Every morning
>I lay out the pieces of my life
>on your altar
>and watch for fire to descend.

Storm Line Agate—said to relieve a restless or troubled mind and create a feeling of calmness and peace. Symbolizes healing, peace, tranquility and relaxation. Thought to create trust, form deep bonds, and facilitate good communication.

> Psalm 18:6-7, 18-19 TPT: In my distress I cried out to you,
> the delivering God, and from your temple-throne
> you heard my troubled cry,
> and my sobs went right into your heart.
> The earth itself shivered and shook.
> It reeled and rocked before him.
> As the mountains trembled, they melted away,
> for his anger was kindled on my behalf!
> When I was at my weakest, my enemies attacked —
> but the Lord held on to me.
> His love broke open the way,
> and he brought me into a beautiful, broad place.
> He rescued me — because his delight is in me!

Striped Agate—symbolizes compassion, generosity, and a keen sense of justice, restoration, and redemption.

> Isaiah 1:17 NLT: Learn to do good.
> Seek justice.
> Help the oppressed.
> Defend the cause of orphans.
> Fight for the rights of widows.

Tree Agate—symbolizes gentleness and inner peace, said to calm nerves and center you and your environment. Combined with quartz it is said to deepen meditation and prayer.

> Psalm 1:3 NLT: The righteous are like trees
> planted along the riverbank, bearing fruit each season.
> Their leaves never wither, and they prosper in all they do.

Psalm 52:8 NLT: I am like an olive tree, thriving in the house of God. I will always trust in God's unfailing love.

Jeremiah 17:7-8 MSG: But blessed is the man who trusts me, God, the woman who sticks with God. They're like trees replanted in Eden, putting down roots near the rivers—Never a worry through the hottest of summers, never dropping a leaf; Serene and calm through droughts, bearing fresh fruit every season.

White Fire Agate—white agate symbolizes balance, release, courage to trust, and harmony of feminine and masculine. Said to help the body release toxins, build the immune system, improve concentration and analytical frames of mind, as well as release trauma.

1 Corinthians 1:8-9 AMP: And He will also confirm you to the end [keeping you strong and free of any accusation, so that you will be] blameless and beyond reproach in the day [of the return] of our Lord Jesus Christ. God is faithful [He is reliable, trustworthy and ever true to His promise—He can be depended on], and through Him you were called into fellowship with His Son, Jesus Christ our Lord.

Alabaster

Genuine alabaster is a soft, translucent form of gypsum and symbolizes purity, transparency, protection, and worship. It is said to draw forgiveness and compassion. Two miles of reliefs carved in alabaster and used to adorn palace walls have been discovered in the ruins of Nineveh. Of course, alabaster is most commonly recalled in the anointing story of Jesus by the sinful woman. Note: Alabaster "beads" are in fact glass beads made to imitate alabaster as genuine alabaster is not durable enough for beads used in jewelry making.

Matthew 26:7-13 NLT: While he was eating, a woman came in with a beautiful alabaster jar of expensive perfume and poured it over his head. The disciples were indignant when they saw this. "What a waste!" they said. "It could have been sold for a high price and the money given to the poor."
    But Jesus, aware of this, replied, "Why criticize this woman for doing such a good thing to me? You will always have the poor among you, but you will not always have me. She has poured this perfume on me to prepare my body for burial. I tell you the truth, wherever the Good News is preached throughout the world, this woman's deed will be remembered and discussed."

Amazonite

With its soft colors of the sea, amazonite is soothing, balancing, centering—increasing harmony and love for all. Said to help with electromagnetic pollution from devices around you. While it comes in a rainbow of colors, the soft blue and green colors are the most prized.

Isaiah 40:12-13a NIV: Who has measured the waters in the hollow of his hand, or with the breadth of his hand marked off the heavens? …Who can fathom the Spirit of the LORD, or instruct the LORD as his counselor?

Amber

With the ancient name "electrum," amber is the solidified and fossilized resin of pine trees. It is one of the oldest gemstones and has been found in tombs from the Stone Age. Ambers that contained insects were most prized among ancient people. It is a grounding, stabilizing, and healing stone symbolic of our connection to creation. With its warm and sunny color it brings an uplifting and joyful energy that is thought to be a natural anti-depressant.

Ezekiel 1:26-28 NLT: Above this surface was something that looked like a throne made of blue lapis lazuli. And on this throne high above was a figure whose appearance resembled a man. From what appeared to be his waist up, he looked like gleaming amber, flickering like a fire. And from his waist down, he looked like a burning flame, shining with splendor. All around him was a glowing halo, like a rainbow shining in the clouds on a rainy day. This is what the glory of the Lord looked like to me.

Amethyst

Forming in geodes and generally found in clusters of crystal points, amethyst is symbolic of balance, wisdom, and discernment, aiding in smooth transitions as you search for God's next steps in your life, and giving you fresh inspiration and a new zestful enthusiasm for life. It is often misstated that the presence of manganese in the stone produces its color, but tests have failed to verify this. Some believe the internal structure of minutely thin layers that bend and fracture the light in different directions is what contributes to its colors. A stone symbolizing spiritual protection, healing, purification, cleansing of negative influences and attachments, amethyst is thought to aid in addiction recovery.

Proverbs 3:1-6 NLT: My child, never forget the things I have taught you. Store my commands in your heart. If you do this, you will live many years, and your life will be satisfying. Never let loyalty and kindness leave you! Tie them around your neck as a reminder. Write them deep within your heart. Then you will find favor with both God and people, and you will earn a good reputation. Trust in the Lord with all your heart; do not depend on your own understanding. Seek his will in all you do, and he will show you which path to take.

Dog Teeth Amethyst—its purple and white striped appearance is due to its combination of amethyst and white quartz. The name derives from the recurring chevron or "dog teeth" pattern of the stripes. Dog teeth amethyst is thought to help soften resistance to change and dispel negativity.

Nehemiah 1:9-10 VOICE: But if you have a change of heart and return to Me and walk according to My commands, then no matter how far you have gone, even to the places beyond the horizon, I will gather you and bring you to the place of My choosing, where My very name dwells."

Lavender Amethyst—a transparent lavender variety of amethyst, it is symbolic of protective light and love.

> Psalm 144:1-2 NIV: Praise be to the Lord my Rock,
> who trains my hands for war, my fingers for battle.
> He is my loving God and my fortress, my stronghold
> and my deliverer, my shield, in whom I take refuge.

Phantom Amethyst—"phantom" crystals are ones that have another crystal inside, giving the appearance of a wispy, smoke-like creature within.

> Psalm 50:2-3a NLT: From Mount Zion, the perfection of
> beauty, God shines in glorious radiance.
> Our God approaches, and he is not silent.

Angelite

As it is believed to deepen attunement, heighten perception and provide protection for the environment or the body, angelite is a powerfully symbolic stone for healers. Said to promote communication and self-expression and, therefore, to help you speak your truth.

Proverbs 4:20-23 NLT: My child, pay attention to what I say.
Listen carefully to my words.
Don't lose sight of them.
Let them penetrate deep into your heart,
for they bring life to those who find them,
and healing to their whole body.
Guard your heart above all else,
for it determines the course of your life.

Aquamarine

A member if the beryl family, aquamarine symbolizes the purity of crystalline waters and the exhilaration and relaxation of the sea. According to *Gems and Minerals of the Bible*, "Historians have likened it to a thousand leagues of sunlit sea imprisoned in a cup" (18). It is calming, soothing, and cleansing, and inspires truth, trust, and letting go. In ancient lore, aquamarine was believed to be the treasure of mermaids and was used by sailors as a talisman of good luck, fearlessness, and protection.

Colossians 2:12 VOICE: You were buried with Him beneath the waters of the ceremonial washing called baptism and then were raised up with Him by faith in the resurrection power of God, who brought Him back from the dead.

Aventurine

Called a "stone of prosperity," aventurine symbolizes leadership and decisiveness, promoting compassion, empathy and perseverance. Said to block electromagnetic waves. It comes in many colors, including green, blue, red, brown and peach.

Joshua 3:7 NLT: The Lord told Joshua, "Today I will begin to make you a great leader in the eyes of all the Israelites. They will know that I am with you, just as I was with Moses."

Green Aventurine—symbolizes comfort, healing, and harmony. It is said to bring things back into alignment, especially following malignancy.

2 Corinthians 1:3-5 MSG: All praise to the God and Father of our Master, Jesus the Messiah! Father of all mercy! God of all healing counsel! He comes alongside us when we go through hard times, and before you know it, he brings us alongside someone else who is going through hard times so that we can be there for that person just as God was there for us. We have plenty of hard times that come from following the Messiah, but no more so than the good times of his healing comfort—we get a full measure of that, too.

Peach Aventurine—said to help with anxiety, worry, stress, and shyness. Symbolizes calmness, balance, and tolerance. Said to stabilize the mind, promote creativity, and increase perception.

I Corinthians 2:15-16 TPT: Those who live in the Spirit are able to carefully evaluate all things, and they are subject to the scrutiny of no one but God. For who has ever intimately known the mind of the Lord Yahweh well enough to become his counselor? Christ has, and we possess Christ's perceptions.

Bloodstone

Bloodstone most commonly refers to green Jasper with red inclusions consisting of Hematite. Bloodstone was known in antiquity as heliotrope, the Sun Stone. It has been treasured for its beauty throughout history. A stone symbolizing courage, purification, and noble sacrifice, it has a long history of use for its healing properties. It has been considered a somewhat magical stone because it is thought to transmute negative energy and purify a space while protecting it at the same time. As Christians we know that it is only the Blood of Jesus that purifies and protects at the same time.

> Isaiah 53:4-5 NIV: Surely he took up our pain and bore our suffering, yet we considered him punished by God, stricken by him, and afflicted. But he was pierced for our transgressions, he was crushed for our iniquities; the punishment that brought us peace was on him, and by his wounds we are healed.

Ephesians 1:6-8 NLT: So we praise God for the glorious grace he has poured out on us who belong to his dear Son. He is so rich in kindness and grace that he purchased our freedom with the blood of his Son and forgave our sins. He has showered his kindness on us, along with all wisdom and understanding.

Bronzite

Called a "Stone of Courtesy," bronzite is said to be helpful to people who greet and assist the public. Symbolizes a loving and unprejudiced discernment within; a polite nature in you and in all you meet; and the ability to resolve unsettled emotions in our life.

> Psalm 18:32-36 VOICE: He teaches me to fight so that my arms can bend a bronze bow. You have shielded me with Your salvation, supporting me with Your strong right hand, and it makes me strong.

Carnelian

Carnelian has many names: Singer's Stone, Sunset Stone and the Artist's Stone because it symbolizes a vivacious creative edge in everything one does. The warm hues of autumn are a reminder to let go of the things that don't serve you, to store warmth and light within the body, and to journey forth, no matter how dim the path. Full of life force and vitality, it is said that carnelian heals the body, mind, and soul. Carnelian was also called sardius in ancient times.

Psalm 119:33-40 MSG: God, teach me lessons for living so I can stay the course. Give me insight so I can do what you tell me— my whole life one long, obedient response. Guide me down the road of your commandments; I love traveling this freeway! Give me a bent for your words of wisdom, and not for piling up loot. Divert my eyes from toys and trinkets, invigorate me on the pilgrim way. Affirm your promises to me—promises made to all who fear you. Deflect the harsh words of my critics—but what you say is always so good. See how hungry I am for your counsel; preserve my life through your righteous ways!

Cat's Eye

In ancient lore, wearing cat's eye was believed to help ward off evil and act as a talisman to protect against unforeseen danger. Symbolizes wealth and prosperity, as well as good judgment, understanding, intuition, and concentration.

> Proverbs 2:8-11 VOICE: He acts as a shield for those who value integrity. God protects the paths of those who pursue justice, watching over the lives of those who keep faith with Him. With this wisdom you will be able to choose the right road, seek justice, and decide what is good and fair. Because wisdom will penetrate deep within and knowledge will become a good friend to your soul. Sound judgment will stand guard over you, and understanding will watch over you as the Lord promised.

Chalcedony

Often found in volcanic rocks, deposited there by circulating groundwater containing silicon dioxide. Chalcedony comes in a variety of colors and symbolizes brotherhood and goodwill, especially in a group setting. Blue chalcedony is a demure crystal—subtle, cool and serene, ethereal yet solid. It has an inviting, soft blue translucence, and an almost imperceptible movement within the stone that invokes a stillness of silent reverence. A stone of peace, peace-making and peace-keeping, it's calming, and speaks of a like-minded spirit and trust in one another.

I Thessalonians 5:23-24 VOICE: So now, may the God of peace make you His own completely and set you apart from the rest. May your spirit, soul, and body be preserved, kept intact and wholly free from any sort of blame at the coming of our Lord Jesus the Anointed. For the God who calls you is faithful, and He can be trusted to make it so.

Chrysocolla

Said to be a peaceful and stabilizing stone, it emphasizes the power our words and actions have on those around us and encourages compassion and strengthening of character. Symbolic of clear communication, gifted teaching, and total transformation.

Proverbs 17:27 AMP: He who has knowledge restrains and is careful with his words. And a man of understanding and wisdom has a cool spirit (self-control, an even temper).

Chrysoprase

Called the stone of Venus, it is the most rare and valuable rich apple-green gemstone in the chalcedony family and was often mistaken for emeralds by ancient jewelers. Unlike emeralds, which owe their color to the presence of chromium, the bright spring green of chrysoprase is a result of trace amounts of nickel. Traditionally symbolized happiness, enterprise, prudence, good fortune, creativity, and prosperity. It is thought to instill you with peace, poise, and grace and help you to recognize the gentle beauty within yourself so you can enjoy self-expression and courage through fluent speech and clarity of thought. Said to encourage non-judgmental attitudes, helping you avoid speaking out unthinkingly in anger.

James 1:17-21 NLT: Whatever is good and perfect is a gift coming down to us from God our Father, who created all the lights in the heavens. He never changes or casts a shifting shadow. He chose to give birth to us by giving us his true word. And we, out of all creation, became his prized possession. Understand this, my dear brothers and sisters: You must all be quick to listen, slow to speak, and slow to get angry. Human anger does not produce the righteousness God desires. So get rid of all the filth and evil in your lives, and humbly accept the word God has planted in your hearts, for it has the power to save your souls.

Citrine

Due to its color, it is said to carry the power of the sun, imparting joy and dispelling gloom and negativity. A cleansing and regenerating stone, it is warming, energizing, and thought to increase creativity, prosperity and generosity.

> Psalm 136:4-5 MSG: Thank the miracle-working God,
> *His love never quits.*
> The God whose skill formed the cosmos,
> *His love never quits.*
> The God who laid out earth on ocean foundations,
> *His love never quits.*
> The God who filled the skies with light, *His love never quits.*
> The sun to watch over the day, *His love never quits.*

Coral

Once a living organism found in the ocean (called a polyp), it has an organic origin despite being referred to as a stone. Coral is one of two gems provided by the sea (the other is pearl), from the branching skeletons of small marine animals. While most coral is white, impurities absorbed by the creatures give them the unique colors of red and blue.

Blue Coral—symbolizes protection, healing, and increased communication. In ancient times, blue fabric and gems were sought after, considered beautiful and valuable, and were used throughout the Temple. Blue is often used to represent the Holy Spirit, healing, and Living Water.

John 4:13-14 AMP: Jesus answered her, "Everyone who drinks this water will be thirsty again. But whoever drinks the water that I give him will never be thirsty again. But the water that I give him will become in him a spring of water [satisfying his thirst for God] welling up [continually flowing, bubbling within him] to eternal life."

Fossil Coral—said to be a lucky stone believed to draw luck and attract wealth. It is also a protection stone which people thought would ward off evil. Symbolizes purity, gentleness, nourishment, protection, and a loving heart.

Titus 3:4-7 AMP: But when the goodness and loving kindness of God our Savior appeared, he saved us, not because of works done by us in righteousness, but according to his own mercy, by the washing of regeneration and renewal of the Holy Spirit, whom he poured out on us richly through Jesus Christ our Savior, so that being justified by his grace we might become heirs according to the hope of eternal life.

Red Coral—said to push back sadness and depression. With its fiery red energy, it symbolizes willpower, strength, and motivation. Red also represents the blood covering of Jesus.

Isaiah 50:7-9 NLT: Because the Sovereign Lord helps me,
I will not be disgraced. Therefore, I have set my face like a
stone, determined to do his will. And I know that I will not
be put to shame. He who gives me justice is near.
Who will dare to bring charges against me now?
Where are my accusers? Let them appear!
See, the Sovereign Lord is on my side!
Who will declare me guilty?
All my enemies will be destroyed!

Diamond

Crystallized carbon, diamonds are the hardest known gem. When transparent and without flaws, they're highly valued, but common diamonds are used as record needles and blades for circular saws. Due to its hardness, it is a symbol of power, fearlessness and an unbreakable spirit—and of course, eternal love!

Note: Although often listed as one of the jewels on Aaron's breastplate, in Biblical times diamonds were more likely only used industrially not for jewelry and decorative use. In fact, you don't find diamonds among the treasure of ancient kings!

> Jeremiah 31:3-4 NIV: The Lord appeared to us in the past, saying: "I have loved you with an everlasting love; I have drawn you with unfailing kindness. I will build you up again, and you, Virgin Israel, will be rebuilt. Again you will take up your timbrels and go out to dance with the joyful.

Emerald

More than twenty times rarer than diamonds, emeralds are the apex of the beryl family. While internal discolorations, cloudiness and fractures mar the possibility of a flawless emerald, their color and rarity make them more expensive than diamonds. According to *Gems and Minerals of the Bible*, "History records that Julius Caesar fancied emeralds because he believed they had potent curative powers" (57). With its deep, cool, verdant green coloration, it symbolizes tranquility, balance, regeneration, healing, and wisdom.

> Job 28:12-18 MSG: But where, oh where, will they find Wisdom? Where does Insight hide?
> Mortals don't have a clue,
> haven't the slightest idea where to look.
> Earth's depths say, "It's not here;"
> ocean deeps echo, "Never heard of it."
> It can't be bought with the finest gold;
> no amount of silver can get it.
> Even famous Ophir gold can't buy it,
> not even diamonds and sapphires.
> Neither gold nor emeralds are comparable;
> extravagant jewelry can't touch it.
> Pearl necklaces and ruby bracelets—why bother?
> None of this is even a down payment on Wisdom!

Flourite

Comes in a variety of colors but is best known for its translucent coloration of lavender and cool green. Fluorite is said to be an excellent learning aid, increasing concentration, self-confidence, and decision-making. A protective stone, it is thought to absorb and neutralize negative energy and stress, encouraging positivity, and balancing energy. Symbolizes balance and coordination—mentally, spiritually, and physically.

> Proverbs 1:5-7 NLT: Let the wise listen to these proverbs
> and become even wiser.
> Let those with understanding receive guidance
> by exploring the meaning in these proverbs and parables,
> the words of the wise and their riddles.
> Fear of the Lord is the foundation of true knowledge,
> but fools despise wisdom and discipline.

Garnet

Garnet symbolizes love and friendship. Associated with the heart, blood, inner fire, and life force, garnets have long been considered symbols of love. Garnets were said to protect travelers on their journeys and were often exchanged between friends as tokens that they would meet again some day.

Philippians 1:3-11 VOICE: Whenever you cross my mind, I thank my God for you and for the gift of knowing you. My spirit is lightened with joy whenever I pray for you (and I do constantly) because you have partnered with me to spread the gospel since the first day I preached to you.

   I am confident that the Creator, who has begun such a great work among you, will not stop in mid-design but will keep perfecting you until the day Jesus the Anointed, our Liberating King, returns to redeem the world. It is only right that I should feel such admiration for you all—you hold me close to your hearts. And, since we are partners in this great work of grace, you have never failed to stand with me as I have defended and stood firm for the gospel… Before God I want you to know how much I long to see you and love you with the affection of the Anointed One, Jesus. And here's what I pray for you:

Father, may their love grow more and more in wisdom and insight—so they will be able to examine and determine the best from everything else. And on the day of the Anointed One, the day of His judgment, let them stand pure and blameless, filled with the fruit of righteousness that ripens through Jesus the Anointed. All this I pray, with a view to God's ultimate praise and glory.

Gold Sandstone or "Goldstone"

An artificially produced stone created by melting silica, copper oxide, and other chemicals that reduce copper to its element form. Called the "Stone of Ambition," it symbolizes determination to help one achieve their goals. A calming, healing, and revitalizing stone said to stabilize emotions and to reduce pain for those with arthritis (due to its copper content).

Job 28:5-8 AMP: [As for] the earth, out of it comes food, But underneath [its surface, down deep] it is turned over as fire. Its stones are the bed of sapphires; It holds dust of gold.

Hematite

Hematite is said to be calming and grounding and to aid in mental organization and focus. With its high iron content (70%), it symbolizes strength, courage, and belief in one's own convictions.

2 Timothy 1:7 AMP: For God did not give us a spirit of timidity or cowardice or fear, but [He has given us a spirit] of power and of love and of sound judgment and personal discipline [abilities that result in a calm, well-balanced mind and self-control].

Howlite

Called a "Guardian Stone," howlite symbolizes self-awareness, increased patience, and the release of attachments to old emotional pain. This marbled stone is said to calm melancholy states of mind and emotion. Also said to relieve insomnia and ease stress and anxiety. The stone is white or cream and is often dyed turquoise color to produce a more affordable version of "turquoise."

Revelation 2:17 ESV: To the one who conquers I will give some of the hidden manna, and I will give him a white stone, with a new name written on the stone that no one knows except the one who receives it.

Iolite

Also known as "The Viking's Compass," iolite displays a visual property called "pleochroism," meaning it can appear to be different colors as it shifts in the light. According to Norse legend, Viking explorers used thin pieces of iolite as the world's first polarizing lens to help them determine the exact location of the sun on cloudy days for navigation. Said to symbolize curiosity and guidance on the journey of spiritual growth and discovery.

John 16:13 AMP: But when He, the Spirit of Truth, comes, He will guide you into all the truth [full and complete truth]. For He will not speak on His own initiative, but He will speak whatever He hears [from the Father—the message regarding the Son], and He will disclose to you what is to come [in the future].

Jade

The name "jade" is applied to two different minerals: nephrite and jadeite. Jade carries a sweet, light, and nourishing energy that can feel very healing. With a soothing purity about it, it goes about purifying your heart in a very accepting, loving, and wise kind of way. Another meaning of jade is gentleness and nourishment because jade is a stone that protects and supports a loving heart. Jade may help you feel like an ancient sage that is so centered in his or her own being and accepting of others that others feel elevated and nurtured just being around you. The message of jade is "Love and Accept Yourself," and its powerful healing starts by helping you align yourself with harmony and balance.

African Jade—a nephrite jade whose bright green coloration is due to traces of chromium.

Jeremiah 33:6 NIV: I will bring health and healing to it; I will heal my people and will let them enjoy abundant peace and security.

Burmese Jade—a variety of jadeite found in Burma and sought after all over the world. Some say is cures pains in the side of the body and is thought to possess health-strengthening properties and assist in fertility and childbirth. Symbolizes longevity and vitality.

Malachi 4:2 NLT: But for you who fear my name, the Sun of Righteousness will rise with healing in his wings. And you will go free, leaping with joy like calves let out to pasture.

Dragon Blood Jade—this variety of jade is the green color of jade we know and love with surprising speckles of red color. The greens vary and unite with red inclusions the striking color of crimson. Green represents healing, and red the blood covering of Jesus.

Ephesians 4:15-16 MSG: We take our lead from Christ, who is the source of everything we do. He keeps us in step with each other. His very breath and blood flow through us, nourishing us so that we will grow up healthy in God, robust in love.

Green Jade—green is the most common color of jade and represents healing.

Matthew 9:35 NIV: Jesus went through all the towns and villages, teaching in their synagogues, proclaiming the good news of the kingdom and healing every disease and sickness.

Honey Jade—a "Stone of Joy & Happiness," it symbolizes creativity, mental agility, practicality, wisdom, love, and tolerance. It is also said to have a balancing and harmonizing effect, banishing negative thoughts and rejuvenating the wearer during times of stress.

Psalm 19:10 NLT: [Your words] are more desirable than gold, even the finest gold. They are sweeter than honey, even honey dripping from the comb.

Red Jade—symbolizes physical vitality, passion, strength, insight, wisdom, knowledge, creativity, and the power of Jesus within. Many cultures consider jade a protective talisman that will assure you of a great life. We know it is the power of Jesus' blood and resurrection that is our true protection…. there is power in the name of Jesus!

Leviticus 17:11 NLT: For the life of the body is in its blood. I have given you the blood on the altar to purify you, making you right with the Lord. It is the blood, given in exchange for a life, that makes purification possible.

Matthew 26:27-28 ESV: And he took a cup, and when he had given thanks he gave it to them, saying, "Drink of it, all of you, for this is my blood of the covenant, which is poured out for many for the forgiveness of sins."

Jasper

The unique artistry of Jasper is that of nature itself—golden sunshine, a nighttime sky, poppy fields, a deep green forest, desert sands, the undulating ocean, red rock canyons, sweeping mountains, even a warm cup of coffee swirling with sweet cream. Each stone is a masterpiece of the Creator. As you will see, varieties of jaspers are plentiful with their names often reflecting their predominant qualities or where they are mined.

Jasper is believed to help one be more present in the physical body and conscious of one's surroundings. Known as the "Supreme Nurturer," it is a stone of protection, grounding, and stability, symbolizing comfort and security, strength and healing, wholeness and peace. Soothing, balancing, and grounding—like a deep breath for the soul—it acts as a reminder that one is not here on earth for oneself, but to bring joy, courage, and wisdom to others. It carries with it the knowledge that it is impossible to give all of one's energy and love because the source (God) of energy and love is never-ending and is always accessible and is constantly replenished.

> Psalm 8:3 TPT: Look at the splendor of your skies,
> your creative genius glowing in the heavens.
> When I gaze at your moon and your stars,
> mounted like jewels in their settings,
> I know you are the fascinating artist who fashioned it all!

> Psalm 146:5-6 NLT: Joyful are those who
> have the God of Israel as their helper,
> whose hope is in the Lord their God.
> He made heaven and earth,
> the sea, and everything in them.
> He keeps every promise forever.

African Kambaba Jasper—formed by a stromatolite (a clump of algae) that fossilized over time turning it into this stromatolite jasper found in Africa. Symbolizes a sense of peace, tranquility, and calmness.

John 14:27 NLT: Jesus said, "I am leaving you with a gift—peace of mind and heart. And the peace I give is a gift the world cannot give. So don't be troubled or afraid."

Apple Jasper—said to aid in grounding and protection. Red represents the blood covering of Jesus Christ. It is also symbolic of protection, courage, energy, and love.

Romans 5:9-11 MSG: Now that we are set right with God by means of this sacrificial death, the consummate blood sacrifice, there is no longer a question of being at odds with God in any way. If, when we were at our worst, we were put on friendly terms with God by the sacrificial death of his Son, now that we're at our best, just think of how our lives will expand and deepen by means of his resurrection life! Now that we have actually received this amazing friendship with God, we are no longer content to simply say it in plodding prose. We sing and shout our praises to God through Jesus, the Messiah!

Aqua Terra Jasper—the name means "water and earth." Said to bring inner peace, clarity, love, and compassion, as well as healing and protection.

Isaiah 51:10-11 NIV: Was it not you who dried up the sea, the waters of the great deep, who made a road in the depths of the sea so that the redeemed might cross over? Those the Lord has rescued will return. They will enter Zion with singing; everlasting joy will crown their heads. Gladness and joy will overtake them, and sorrow and sighing will flee away.

Artistic Jasper—made up of calcite or calcium carbonate, artistic jasper has beautiful, intricate patterns of minute black flecks, bands, and veins within tan, cream, gray, and mauve stones.

> Isaiah 64:8 NIV: Yet still, Yahweh, you are our Father.
> We are like clay and you are our Potter.
> Each one of us is the creative, artistic work of your hands.

Australian Butter Jasper—an opaque yellow-green stone with beige or grey inclusions. Protective, nurturing, and healing.

> Psalm 91: 4 VOICE: Like a bird protecting its young,
> God will cover you with His feathers,
> will protect you under His great wings;
> His faithfulness will form a shield around you,
> a rock-solid wall to protect you.

Australian Jasper (aka Mookaite)—symbolizes beauty, adventure, grounding, and centering. Mookaite is a healing stone that helps provide stability to one's perspective of life, helping to make right decisions based on objective knowledge, personal power, and willpower.

> Proverbs 2:2-11 NLT: Tune your ears to wisdom and concentrate on understanding. Cry out for insight and ask for understanding. Search for them as you would for silver; seek them like hidden treasures. Then you will understand what it means to fear the Lord, and you will gain knowledge of God. For the Lord grants wisdom! From his mouth come knowledge and understanding. He grants a treasure of common sense to the honest. He is a shield to those who walk with integrity. He guards the paths of the just and protects those who are faithful to him. Then you will understand what is right, just, and fair, and you will find the right way to go. For wisdom will enter your heart, and knowledge will fill you with joy. Wise choices will watch over you. Understanding will keep you safe.

Brecciated Jasper—the jagged pattern gives the stone the name "brecciated," which means broken.

Mark 14:3 NIV: While Jesus was in Bethany, reclining at the table in the home of Simon the Leper, a woman came with an alabaster jar of very expensive perfume, made of pure nard. She broke the jar and poured the perfume on his head. (Note: We also know that Jesus himself was broken and poured out as he gave his life on the cross. This is also foreshadowed by Jesus in the breaking of bread and offering of the cup at the Last Supper.)

Dalmatian Jasper—symbolizing positivity, happiness, and childlike playfulness, it is said to help break down barriers you have created around yourself, helping you to move forward in life.

Matthew 18:2-5 MSG: For an answer Jesus called over a child, whom he stood in the middle of the room, and said, "I'm telling you, once and for all, that unless you return to square one and start over like children, you're not even going to get a look at the kingdom, let alone get in. Whoever becomes simple and elemental again, like this child, will rank high in God's kingdom. What's more, when you receive the childlike on my account, it's the same as receiving me."

Fossil Jasper—symbolizing protection and grounding, it instills a feeling of wholeness, healing, serenity, mental clarity, and being cared for.

> Psalm 7:10 TPT: God, your wrap-around presence is my protection and my defense. You bring victory to all who reach out for you.

Golden Creek Jasper—symbolizes balance, relaxation, happiness, tranquility, compassion, and self-discipline.

> Psalm 40:16 VOICE: But may all who look for You discover true joy and happiness in You;
> May those who cherish how You save them always say, "O Eternal One, You are great *and are first in our hearts.*"

Impression Jasper—a low quality variscite (hydrated aluminum phosphate) often dyed to create bright colors not naturally found in nature.

Psalm 139:17-18 VOICE: Your thoughts and plans are treasures to me, O God! I cherish each and every one of them! How grand in scope! How many in number! If I could count each one of them, they would be more than all the grains of sand on earth. Their number is inconceivable! Even when I wake up, I am still near to You.

Iron Zebra Jasper—motivating, mood lifting, and energetic, as well as grounding, centering, and strengthening. It is said to be good for meditation and spiritual work. It encourages a generous, loving interpretation of the people in your life, helping you see beneath the superficial to see their true nature in a loving light.

Ephesians 5:1-2, 8-10 AMP: Therefore become imitators of God [copy Him and follow His example], as well-beloved children [imitate their father]; and walk continually in love [that is, value one another—practice empathy and compassion, unselfishly seeking the best for others], just as Christ also loved you and gave Himself up for us, an offering and sacrifice to God [slain for you, so that it became] a sweet fragrance. For once you were darkness, but now you are light in the Lord; walk as children of Light [live as those who are native-born to the Light] (for the fruit [the effect, the result] of the Light consists in all goodness and righteousness and truth), trying to learn [by experience] what is pleasing to the Lord.

Kiwi Jasper—a warm, nurturing stone. Said to be a good stone for healing, especially when praying for healing on the behalf of others, and also for people in counseling or therapy, who want to overcome addictions or compulsive behavior and gather up strength for the battles ahead. It is also symbolic of power, courage, and strength for those who stand for justice and fairness.

> Isaiah 61:7-9 VOICE: Many called you disgraced and defiled and said that shame should be your share of things.
> Yet you suffered doubly and lived in disgrace;
> so DOUBLE will be your share, and with JOY everlasting.
> *For I, the Eternal One, love justice.*
> I hate stealing and all manner of wrongdoing. In faithfulness to those who do justice, I promise they will be rewarded for their work; and I will establish an everlasting covenant with them. Furthermore, I will promise them My support for their children, so that all nations and everyone around will see that they are the children blessed by the Eternal God.

Leopard Speck Jasper—a stone of tranquility, it unifies and aligns mind, body, and soul, absorbs negative energy, aids quick thinking, and re-energizes after an illness.

Ecclesiastes 5:20 AMP: For he will not often consider the [troubled] days of his life, because God keeps him occupied and focused on the joy of his heart [and the tranquility of God indwells him].

Mahogany Jasper—symbolic of protection, courage, love, strength, physical energy, healing, luck, success, and the destruction of disease. Red is also symbolic of the blood covering of Jesus Christ.

Romans 3:24 VOICE: Yet they are now saved and set right by His free gift of grace through the redemption available only in Jesus the Anointed. When God set Him up to be the sacrifice—the seat of mercy where sins are atoned through faith—His blood became the demonstration of God's own restorative justice.

Mexican Red Snowflake Jasper—said to be a powerful protective stone that calms the emotions and cultivates inner strength. A "Warrior Stone," it is symbolic of a strong life force, vibrancy, endurance, stamina, focus, and determination.

Joshua 1:6-9 VOICE: So be strong and courageous, for you will lead this people as they acquire and then divide the land I promised to their ancestors. Always be strong and courageous, and always live by all of the law I gave to my servant Moses, never turning from it—even ever so slightly—so that you may succeed wherever you go. Let the words from the book of the law be always on your lips. Meditate on them day and night so that you may be careful to live by all that is written in it. If you do, as you make your way through this world, you will prosper and always find success. This is My command: be strong and courageous. Never be afraid or discouraged because I am your God, the Eternal One, and I will remain with you wherever you go.

Ocean Jasper—represents joy, healing, and the release of negative feelings. This uplifting stone is believed to help you deal with past events, allowing you to see what you may have previously seen as negative in a new light.

> Isaiah 51:10-11 NIV: Was it not you who dried up the sea,
> the waters of the great deep,
> who made a road in the depths of the sea
> so that the redeemed might cross over?
> Those the Lord has rescued will return.
> They will enter Zion with singing;
> everlasting joy will crown their heads.
> Gladness and joy will overtake them,
> and sorrow and sighing will flee away.

Picasso Jasper—said to attract positive people into one's life and to support and encourage friendships to blossom in healthy loving ways, and also help renew old friendships that may have been lost. It has strong grounding and calming quality that helps to encourage strength and self-discipline.

> Proverbs 18:24 AMP: The man of too many friends [chosen indiscriminately] will be broken in pieces and come to ruin, But there is a [true, loving] friend who [is reliable and] sticks closer than a brother.

Picture Jasper—said to be a "Stone of Wisdom," picture jasper speaks through creative pictures found in the stone's landscape-like markings. Aids in creative visualization and brings a sense of proportion and harmony to one's understanding of these messages. Represents comfort and the alleviation of fear as one examines current and past issues.

Joel 2:28 NIV: And afterward, I will pour out my Spirit on all people. Your sons and daughters will prophesy, your old men will dream dreams, your young men will see visions.

Polychrome Jasper—said to be a healing stone that creates a comforting feeling of safety, security, and happy thoughts. Represents awakening to new hopefulness, happiness, and joy in your life.

Philippians 4:6-8 VOICE: Don't be anxious about things; instead, pray. Pray about everything. He longs to hear your requests, so talk to God about your needs and be thankful for what has come. And know that the peace of God (a peace that is beyond any and all of our human understanding) will stand watch over your hearts and minds in Jesus, the Anointed One. Finally, brothers and sisters, fill your minds with beauty and truth. Meditate on whatever is honorable, whatever is right, whatever is pure, whatever is lovely, whatever is good, whatever is virtuous and praiseworthy.

Porcelain Jasper—a stone of nurturing gentleness and calm relaxation, it symbolizes stability, safety, security, and emotional protection when dealing with difficult and sensitive issues.

Matthew 11:29 AMP: Take my yoke upon you and learn from me {following me as my disciple], for I am gentle and humble at heart, and you will find rest (renewal, blessed quiet) for your souls.

Red Silver Mist Jasper—promotes balance, stability, and strength of purpose. Red jasper is also believed to be a stone of strength and endurance.

James 1:2-4 NLT: Dear brothers and sisters, when troubles of any kind come your way, consider it an opportunity for great joy. For you know that when your faith is tested, your endurance has a chance to grow. So let it grow, for when your endurance is fully developed, you will be perfect and complete, needing nothing.

Rocky Butte Jasper—thought to be one of the oldest sediments that originated through the ashes of the volcanic flows. Said to instill creative inspiration; obliterate the root cause of stress; encourage the spirit of brotherhood; bring nobility to every action; help one speak in truth, take action against injustice, and deal with conflict. The colorful hues of this rock combined with "drizzle" or gliding patterns make it quite mesmerizing, and it was thought to reveal hidden meanings of situations and prophetic dreams, and widen the imagination to hold onto their significance.

Psalm 36:5-10 NLT: Your unfailing love, O Lord, is as vast as
the heavens; your faithfulness reaches beyond the clouds.
Your righteousness is like the mighty mountains,
your justice like the ocean depths.
You care for people and animals alike, O Lord.
How precious is your unfailing love, O God!
All humanity finds shelter in the shadow of your wings.

> You feed them from the abundance of your own house,
> letting them drink from your river of delights.
> For you are the fountain of life, the light by which we see.
> Pour out your unfailing love on those who love you;
> give justice to those with honest hearts.

Sea Sediment Jasper—symbolizes stability and protection and is said to ease emotional stress and bring clarity, peace, love, and compassion.

> Psalm 139:17-18 VOICE: Your thoughts and plans
> are treasures to me, O God!
> I cherish each and every one of them!
> How grand in scope!
> How many in number!
> If I could count each one of them,
> they would be more than all the grains of sand on earth.
> Their number is inconceivable!
> Even when I wake up, I am still near to You.

Silver Leaf Jasper (Black)—promotes balance and stability; symbolizes strength of purpose.

Philippians 2:13 AMP: For it is [not your strength, but it is] God who is effectively at work in you, both to will and to work [that is, strengthening, energizing, and creating in you the longing and the ability to fulfill your purpose] for His good pleasure.

Snowflake Jasper—physically and emotionally healing and grounding. With its snowflake pattern, it's a great stone for those who love nature… especially winter!

> Psalm 51:7 NIV: Cleanse me with hyssop,
> and I will be clean;
> wash me,
> and I will be whiter than snow.

Sonora Dendritic Jasper—the story goes that it was discovered in 2009 in Mexico when a man chasing his goat up a mountain caught sight of an unusual rock. The stone's composition remains somewhat ambiguous, as it is softer than both jasper and rhyolite. The best available information indicates that the stone is a type of dolomite that has been altered by volcanic activity. Symbolizes stability in growth and change, encouragement in creativity, and taking pleasure in every moment of life.

Hebrews 10:23-24 TPT: So now we must cling tightly to the hope that lives within us, knowing that God always keeps his promises! Discover creative ways to encourage others and to motivate them toward acts of compassion, doing beautiful works as expressions of love.

Spider Web Jasper—its spider web pattern reminds you of the intricate facets of God's creation and the interconnectedness of all creatures within it. This stone also symbolizes alignment, beauty, and healing, and is said to protect one from the negative energy of others.

Psalm 145:15-21 MSG: All eyes are on you, expectant…
Generous to a fault, you lavish your favor on all creatures.
Everything God does is right—the trademark
on all his works is love.
God's there, listening for all who pray,
for all who pray and mean it.
He does what's best for those who fear him—
hears them call out and saves them.
God sticks by all who love him,
but it's all over for those who don't.
My mouth is filled with God's praise.
Let everything living bless him,
bless his holy name from now to eternity!

Terra Jasper—a beautiful blue-and-brown combination, with some beads resembling little globes of planet Earth—the brown shapes creating new continents aside warm, blue oceans. Said to be a healing stone of comfort, confidence, courage, and the strength of one's convictions.

Genesis 1:9-10 VOICE: Let the waters below the heavens be collected into one place and congregate into one vast sea, so that dry land may appear. And God called the dry land "earth" and the waters congregated below "seas." And God saw that His new creation was beautiful and good.

Venus Jasper—also called orbicular rhyolite, it gets its name from the planet Venus, which got its name from the Roman goddess of love and beauty.

> Psalm 100:5 MSG: For God is sheer beauty; all-generous in love; loyal always and ever.

Wildhorse Picture Jasper—believed to instill a sense of proportion and harmony, enlivening one's creativity and initiative, and bring hidden emotions to the surface for healing. Picture jaspers are full of masterful scenes in the form of "landscapes patterns"—believed to carry messages from our ancient pasts.

Jeremiah 6:16 NIV: This is what the Lord says: "Stand at the crossroads and look; ask for the ancient paths, ask where the good way is, and walk in it, and you will find rest for your souls."

Wood Jasper—symbolizes healthy roots and a healthy body; said to help one develop a strong back.

Jeremiah 17:8 ESV: He is like a tree planted by water, that sends out its roots by the stream, and does not fear when heat comes, for its leaves remain green, and is not anxious in the year of drought, for it does not cease to bear fruit.

Zebra Jasper—with stripes like a zebra, it is obvious where this jasper gets its name. The bigger question—is it black with white stripes or white with black stripes? See Iron Zebra Jasper for more.

Matthew 16:24-25 MSG: Jesus said, "Anyone who intends to come with me has to let me lead. You're not in the driver's seat; I am. Don't run from suffering; embrace it. Follow me and I'll show you how. Self-help is no help at all. Self-sacrifice is the way, my way, to finding yourself, your true self."

Kyanite

Kyanite means "blue," and this stone is said to help you promote inner balance, clear negativity, trust your intuition and inner wisdom, and find peace. It is also said to help you "speak your truth." Blue is symbolic of all things heavenly and of God's Holy Spirit.

John 14:27 AMP: Peace I leave with you; My [perfect] peace I give to you; not as the world gives do I give to you. Do not let your heart be troubled, nor let it be afraid. [Let My perfect peace calm you in every circumstance and give you courage and strength for every challenge.]

Labradorite

Lore of the Inuit people claims labradorite fell from the frozen fire of the Aurora Borealis. An ordinary stone that transforms to the extraordinary, its iridescent, reflective quality attributes to it being called the most powerful protector of the mineral kingdom. It is said to create a shield against the negativity of this world and strengthen natural energy from within, especially for all who travel and embrace the world seeking knowledge and guidance from God.

Proverbs 4:5-6 AMP: Get [skillful and godly] wisdom!
Acquire understanding [actively seek spiritual discernment,
mature comprehension, and logical interpretation]!
Do not forget nor turn away from the words of my mouth.
Do not turn away from [Wisdom]
and she will guard and protect you;
Love her, and she will watch over you.

Lapis Lazuli

Lapis lazuli has been found adorning the tombs, caskets, and mummies of many ancient peoples. It has long been a symbol of royalty and wealth. Its deep, celestial blue is also a universal symbol of honor, power, vision, wisdom, truth, and for the Christian, the Holy Spirit, who embodies these qualities. Lapis is said to help bring inner peace and clears the mind of negative thought patterns. Like the deep blue ocean, it brings healing to the soul.

Note: In scripture, the word *sappir* (which means "blue") is often translated as the gemstone sapphire, when in reality the stone most likely would have been lapis lazuli (as the oldest blue sapphire deposit was found in Sri Lanka and the term "sapphire from Sri Lanka" wasn't used until 480 BC in Roman literature). You will often see one or the other based on which translation of scripture you are using.

Exodus 24:9-11 NIV: Moses and Aaron, Nadab and Abihu, and the seventy elders of Israel went up and saw the God of Israel. Under his feet was something like a pavement made of **lapis lazuli,** as bright blue as the sky. But God did not raise his hand against these leaders of the Israelites; they saw God, and they ate and drank.

ESV: Then Moses, Aaron, Nadab, and Abihu, and seventy of the elders of Israel went up, and they saw the God of Israel. There was under his feet as it were a pavement of **sapphire stone**, like the very heaven for clearness. And he did not lay his hand on the chief men of the people of Israel; they beheld God and ate and drank.

Larimar

Blue Larimar is a unique variety of pectolite, a stone with unusual fibrous formation. Found only in the Dominican Republic in the Caribbean, it was only discovered in 1916. It forms in cavities within lava created by volcanic eruptions, and its shape is formed of unique needle-like crystals. Its resonance with the waters of the Caribbean Ocean makes it a beautiful symbol of relaxation, stress relief, and peaceful calm.

> Amos 9:6 AMP: It is He who builds His upper chambers in the heavens and has established His vaulted dome
> (the firmament of heaven) over the earth,
> He who calls to the waters of the sea and pours them out on the face of the earth — The Lord is His name.

Lepidolite

With a glassy or lustrous sheen, lepidolite is the most abundant lithium-bearing mineral as well as a significant source of the rare alkali metals rubidium and caesium. Called the "Stress Relief Stone," it is believed to be a soothing, calming stone, and help you if you are feeling anxious, stressed, or depressed. Also believed to aid in decision-making.

> Psalm 131:2 VOICE: Of one thing I am certain:
> my soul has become calm, quiet, and contented in You.
> Like a weaned child resting upon his mother,
> I am quiet.
> My soul is like this weaned child.

Malachite

Due to the toxicity of its dust (which is 70% copper oxide), malachite should only be used in its polished form. A protective and purifying stone thought to increase intuition and insight, it symbolizes transformation, renewal, and rebirth.

> Isaiah 58:11-12 NIV: The Lord will guide you always;
> he will satisfy your needs in a sun-scorched land
> and will strengthen your frame.
> You will be like a well-watered garden,
> like a spring whose waters never fail.
> Your people will rebuild the ancient ruins
> and will raise up the age-old foundations;
> you will be called Repairer of Broken Walls,
> Restorer of Streets with Dwellings.

Moonstone

Moonstone is a member of the feldspar family, which also includes larvikite and labradorite. Used in Roman jewelry nearly 2,000 years ago, it is considered a sacred stone in many countries. It is said to be a stone for "new beginnings." Symbolizing inner growth and strength, it soothes emotional instability and stress. Moonstone enhances intuition, success, inspiration, and good fortune in both love and business.

> Isaiah 43:18-21 TPT: Stop dwelling on the past.
> Don't even remember these former things.
> I am doing something brand new, something unheard of.
> Even now it sprouts and grows and matures.
> Don't you perceive it? I will make a way in the wilderness
> and open up flowing streams in the desert.
> Wild beasts, jackals and owls will glorify me.
> For I supply streams of water in the desert and rivers in the wilderness to satisfy the thirst of my people, my chosen ones, so that you, whom I have shaped and formed for myself, will proclaim my praise.

Norwegian Moonstone (Larvikite)—said to protect you in your waking and sleeping hours, as well as traveling. Symbolizes cleansing—ridding or healing the body of anything that is no longer useful to you. Also said to be a good stone for meditation as it symbolizes the focus and stillness of mind.

Psalm 121 NLT: I look up to the mountains—
does my help come from there?
My help comes from the Lord, who made heaven and earth!
He will not let you stumble;
the one who watches over you will not slumber.
Indeed, he who watches over Israel
never slumbers or sleeps.
The Lord himself watches over you!
The Lord stands beside you as your protective shade.
The sun will not harm you by day, nor the moon at night.
The Lord keeps you from all harm
and watches over your life.
The Lord keeps watch over you as you come and go,
both now and forever.

Peach Moonstone—said to bring soothing relief to emotional issues, such as depression or anger, and to bring emotional support for those who are sensitive and intuitive. Symbolizes a loving energy that brings God into all situations.

Psalm 94:18-19 TPT: When I screamed out,
"Lord, I'm doomed!"
your fiery love was stirred, and you raced to my rescue.
Whenever my busy thoughts were out of control,
the soothing comfort of your presence
calmed me down and overwhelmed me with delight.

Morganite

Powerful and highly vibrational, morganite is a universal stone of unconditional love. A member of the beryl family, whose siblings include emerald and aquamarine, it symbolizes connection to Divine Love (God).

Romans 8:38-39 NLT: And I am convinced that nothing can ever separate us from God's love. Neither death nor life, neither angels nor demons, neither our fears for today nor our worries about tomorrow—not even the powers of hell can separate us from God's love. No power in the sky above or in the earth below—indeed, nothing in all creation will ever be able to separate us from the love of God that is revealed in Christ Jesus our Lord.

Obsidian

A naturally occurring volcanic glass, formed when lava erupts and cools rapidly with minimal crystal growth. Symbolic of truth, protection, compassion, strength, and exploration of the unknown. Believed to help you uncover who you were created to be by uncovering old trauma and emotional blockages.

Jeremiah 51:24-25 AMP: "And I will [completely] repay Babylon and all the people of Chaldea [your enemies] for all the evil that they have done in Zion [and against you]—before your very eyes [I will do it]," says the Lord. "Behold, I am against you, O destroying mountain [conqueror of nations], who destroys the whole earth," declares the Lord, "I will stretch out My hand against you, and roll you down from the [rugged] cliffs, and will make you a burnt mountain [an extinct volcano]."

In this passage, God is speaking out against the enemies of his chosen people. Later in verse 36, God promises, "Behold, I will plead your case and take full vengeance for you." God speaks out and rises up against your enemies and will seek vengeance on your behalf.

Flower or "Snowflake" Obsidian—a naturally occurring volcanic glass believed to dissolve shocks, fears, traumas, and both physical and emotional pain. Like a sky full of beautiful snowflakes, snowflake obsidian restores a deep, abiding sense of protection and reverence.

Job 37:1-6 MSG: "Whenever this happens, my heart stops— I'm stunned, I can't catch my breath. Listen to it! Listen to his thunder, the rolling, rumbling thunder of his voice. He lets loose his lightning from horizon to horizon, lighting up the earth from pole to pole. In their wake, the thunder echoes his voice, powerful and majestic. He lets out all the stops, he holds nothing back. No one can mistake that voice—His word thundering so wondrously, his mighty acts staggering our understanding. He orders the snow, 'Blanket the earth!' and the rain, 'Soak the whole countryside!' No one can escape the weather—it's there. And no one can escape from God.

Onyx

Onyx is one of the oldest stones mentioned in scripture (along with *dbellium* whose meaning is uncertain). As the scripture below indicates, the art of stone engraving has been around since ancient times. It was often used for seals and signet rings. As the scripture indicates, black onyx is represents improved memory and increased analytical talents.

Exodus 28:9-12 MSG: Take two onyx stones and engrave the names of the sons of Israel on them in the order of their birth, six names on one stone and the remaining six on the other. Engrave the names of the sons of Israel on the two stones the way a jeweler engraves a seal. Then mount the stones in settings of filigreed gold. Fasten the two stones on the shoulder pieces of the Ephod—they are memorial stones for the Israelites. Aaron will wear these names on his shoulders as a memorial before God.

Green Onyx—a symbol of purity and restfulness, it is said to relieve you of your worries, fears, tension, and stress. Its green soothing color will give you strong and positive feelings and give you the mental support that you need to make the wisest decisions during times of difficulty.

Proverbs 2:3-11 NLT: Cry out for insight,
and ask for understanding.
Search for them as you would for silver;
seek them like hidden treasures.
Then you will understand what it means to fear the Lord,
and you will gain knowledge of God.
For the Lord grants wisdom!
From his mouth come knowledge and understanding.
He grants a treasure of common sense to the honest.
He is a shield to those who walk with integrity.
He guards the paths of the just
and protects those who are faithful to him.
Then you will understand what is right, just, and fair,
and you will find the right way to go.
For wisdom will enter your heart,
and knowledge will fill you with joy.
Wise choices will watch over you.
Understanding will keep you safe.

Opal

All opals are a form of hydrated amorphous silica, which means they contain water. All opals don't exhibit the vibrant play of color seen in precious opals. In scripture, *dbellium* is one of the first stones mentioned, but its meaning is uncertain. The authors of *Gems and Minerals of the Bible*, based on its usage, believe it could possibly be referring to opal (16).

The Aboriginal tribes of Australia believed opals were God's footprints on earth. Opals symbolize faithfulness and confidence. They are said to control the temper and calm the nerves.

Psalm 37:3-5 AMP: Trust [rely on and have confidence] in the Lord and do good; Dwell in the land and feed [securely] on His faithfulness. Delight yourself in the Lord,
And He will give you the desires and petitions of your heart.
Commit your way to the Lord;
Trust in Him also and He will do it.

Fire Opal—mined in both precious and common forms, it symbolizes luck, abundance, creativity, and passion. Said to enhance intuition and help you make better decisions by encouraging you trust your instincts. Fire Opal is said to bring a zest for variety and spice for your life.

Psalm 66:8-9, 12: Let the whole world bless our God
and loudly sing his praises.
Our lives are in his hands,
and he keeps our feet from stumbling.
You put a leader over us.
We went through fire and flood,
but you brought us to a place of great abundance.

The following are all considered "common opals."

Black Moss Opal—symbolizes connection with your environment, and nature as well as physical and emotional support and growth.

Genesis 2:7-9 AMP: Then the Lord God formed [that is, created the body of] man from the dust of the ground, and breathed into his nostrils the breath of life; and the man became a living being [an individual complete in body and spirit]. And the Lord God planted a garden (oasis) in the east, in Eden (delight, land of happiness); and He put the man whom He had formed (created) there. And [in that garden] the Lord God caused to grow from the ground every tree that is desirable and pleasing to the sight and good (suitable, pleasant) for food; the tree of life was also in the midst of the garden, and the tree of the [experiential] knowledge (recognition) of [the difference between] good and evil.

Blue Gray Opal—gives hope to life; symbolizes physical and emotional support and growth.

Isaiah 58:8 NIV: Then your light will break forth like the dawn, and your healing will quickly appear; then your righteousness will go before you, and the glory of the Lord will be your rear guard.

White African Opal—believed to provide gentle, nurturing emotional support, and symbolize calmness and purity, awakening mental capacities such as creativity, inspiration, imagination, and even facilitate memory.

Romans 15:13 TPT: Now may God, the inspiration and fountain of hope, fill you to overflowing with uncontainable joy and perfect peace as you trust in him. And may the power of the Holy Spirit continually surround your life with his super-abundance until you radiate with hope!

Pearl

Like coral, pearls are another "gem" of the sea! They are symbolic of wisdom, preciousness, rarity, and purity. In aboriginal cultures, they were known as gems of the moon, and great vitality was given to the own who found one in the sparking tropical waters that hid these treasures.

Matthew 10:45-46 TPT: Heaven's kingdom realm is also like a jewel merchant in search of rare pearls. When he discovered one very precious and exquisite pearl, a pearl of great price, he immediately gave up all he had in exchange for it.

Passion Translation Study Note: The Aramaic is "unique." Jesus is the merchant. As his beloved follower, you are the exquisite and unique pearl that came from the wounded side of Jesus Christ. You prompted him to give up all, including his sacred blood, in exchange for having you as his very own.

Pietersite

Golden Pietersite has been called the "Tempest Stone" for its colors of deep blue and gray (forming a stormy sky) with metallic gold and flashes of brilliant bands that catch the light (resembling lightening). Pietersite is composed of Tiger's Eye, Hawk's Eye, and Jasper and symbolizes letting go of negativity.

> Psalm 18:9-12 TPT: He stretched heaven's curtain open and came to my defense.
> Swiftly he rode to earth as the stormy sky was lowered.
> He rode a chariot of thunderclouds amidst thick darkness, a cherub his steed as he swooped down,
> soaring on the wings of Spirit-wind.
> Wrapped and hidden in the thick-cloud darkness, his thunder-tabernacle surrounded him.
> He hid himself in mystery-darkness;
> the dense rain clouds were his garments.
> Suddenly the brilliance of his presence broke through with lightning bolts and with a mighty storm from heaven — like a tempest dropping coals of fire.

Prehnite

Prehnite is said to connect you to the mind of God and, therefore, heighten in you the gift of prophecy. It is symbolic of preparedness, spiritual growth, and wisdom, and is said to link heart and will to help you live from your heart.

1 Corinthians 13:1-3 NLT: If I could speak all the languages of earth and of angels, but didn't love others, I would only be a noisy gong or a clanging cymbal. If I had the gift of prophecy, and if I understood all of God's secret plans and possessed all knowledge, and if I had such faith that I could move mountains, but didn't love others, I would be nothing. If I gave everything I have to the poor and even sacrificed my body, I could boast about it; but if I didn't love others, I would have gained nothing.

Pyrite

Pyrite or "Fool's Gold" was treasured in many ancient civilizations. Pyrite gets its name from the Greek word *pyr*, which means fire. This fiery crystal is a symbol of abundance and prosperity, persistence and commitment, and the strength and determination to take on challenging tasks and make thoughtful business decisions. Like a protective father figure, pyrite shields, protects, and is thought to pass on sound advice, guidance, and wisdom.

Proverbs 15:5 NIV: A fool spurns a parent's discipline, but whoever heeds correction shows prudence.

James 1:16-18 NLT: So, don't be misled, my dear brothers and sisters. Whatever is good and perfect is a gift coming down to us from God our Father, who created all the lights in the heavens. He never changes or casts a shifting shadow. He chose to give birth to us by giving us his true word. And we, out of all creation, became his prized possession.

Quartz

Known as the "master healer" of stones, crystal quartz is one of the most common and abundant gemstones in the world. Symbolizes a heart, mind, and soul open to God's guidance. In its natural form, this clear yet radiant crystal is said to accelerate the fulfillment of the healing process and one's prayers.

Revelation 22:1-5 NIV: Then the angel showed me the river of the water of life, flowing with water *clear as crystal*, continuously pouring out from the throne of God and of the Lamb. The river was flowing in the middle of the street of the city, and on either side of the river was the Tree of Life, with its twelve kinds of ripe fruit according to each month of the year. The leaves of the Tree of Life are for the healing, nurture and care of the nations. And every curse will be broken and no longer exist, for the throne of God and of the Lamb will be there in the city. His loving servants will serve and worship him; they will always see his face, and his name will be on their foreheads. Night will be no more. They will never need the light of the sun or a lamp, because the Lord God will shine on them.

Black Tourmalinated Quartz—this beautiful and unusual crystal combines the healing properties of two gemstones: Quartz Crystal and Black Tourmaline. Clear quartz symbolizes an elevated consciousness, bringing clarity to life as it works as an amplifier. The black tourmaline symbolizes connection and grounding. The melding of these two minerals creates a powerful healing, cleansing, and purifying energy that works together to restore harmony and tranquility.

James 4:8 NLT: Come close to God, and God will come close to you. Wash your hands, you sinners; purify your hearts, for your loyalty is divided between God and the world.

Cherry Quartz—said to restore balance, encourage activity, vitality, and energy of mind, body, and spirit.

> Isaiah 40:28-31 AMP: Do you not know? Have you not heard? The Everlasting God, the Lord, the Creator of the ends of the earth does not become tired or grow weary;
> There is no searching of His understanding.
> He gives strength to the weary,
> and to him who has no might He increases power.
> Even youths grow weary and tired,
> and vigorous young men stumble badly,
> But those who wait for the Lord
> [who expect, look for, and hope in Him]
> Will gain new strength and renew their power;
> They will lift up their wings [and rise up close to God]
> like eagles [rising toward the sun];
> They will run and not become weary;
> They will walk and not grow tired.

Golden Blood Quartz—known as the "Golden Healer," golden blood quartz is said to restore your body's balance and encourage peace and harmony and to fill you with golden healing light. We know the blood of the Jesus, the Light of the World, brings us healing at every level.

1 John 1:7 NIV: But if we walk in the light as He is in the light, we have fellowship with one another, and the blood of Jesus Christ His Son cleanses us from all sin.

Hebrews 1:3 VOICE: This is the One who—imprinted with God's image, shimmering with His glory—sustains all that exists through the power of His word. He was seated at the right hand of God once He Himself had made the offering that purified us from all our sins.

Opalite Quartz—symbolizes all-around healing, stabilizing mood swings, and overcoming tiredness. Said to aid in transitions, encouraging persistence, success, good communication, and strength to honestly speak one's truth.

Ephesians 4:29-30 TPT: And never let ugly or hateful words come from your mouth, but instead let your words become beautiful gifts that encourage others; do this by speaking words of grace to help them. The Holy Spirit of God has sealed you in Jesus Christ until you experience your full salvation. So never grieve the Spirit of God or take for granted his holy influence in your life.

Peach Quartz—symbolizes joy in everyday life, forgiveness, self-respect, independence, creativity, openness to God, and courage to release past issues and traumas. It is said to help one transcend the mundane aspects of life; to connect one's dreams to their reality; and to help when you find it difficult to express yourself emotionally or when you feel that you are lacking in personal power.

2 Chronicles 1:11-12 NIV: God said to Solomon, "Since this is your heart's desire and you have not asked for wealth, possessions or honor, nor for the death of your enemies, and since you have not asked for a long life but for wisdom and

knowledge to govern my people over whom I have made you king, therefore wisdom and knowledge will be given you. And I will also give you wealth, possessions and honor, such as no king who was before you ever had and none after you will have."

Picture Window Quartz—found in its geometric, crystal form—like a window into the heart, mind, and soul—this clear yet radiant crystal is said to accelerate the fulfillment of the healing process and one's prayers.

> Psalm 139:23-24 MSG: Investigate my life, O God, find out everything about me; Cross-examine and test me, get a clear picture of what I'm about; See for yourself whether I've done anything wrong—then guide me
> on the road to eternal life.

Rhodonite Quartz—said to increase feelings of acceptance and forgiveness. Pink represents passion and is a mixture of red (blood of Jesus) and white (holiness).

> Psalm 130:3-4 MSG: If you, God, kept records on wrongdoings, who would stand a chance?
> As it turns out, forgiveness is your habit,
> and that's why you're worshiped.

Rose Quartz—the symbolism of rose quartz is greatly connected to its pink color. Pink represents gentleness, calmness, femininity, compassion, and love. Its gentle energy supports and rekindles relationships, bringing joy, passion, and contentment.

> Galatians 5:22-23 TPT: But the fruit produced by the Holy Spirit within you is divine love in all its varied expressions:
> joy that overflows, peace that subdues,
> patience that endures, kindness in action,
> a life full of virtue, faith that prevails,
> gentleness of heart, and strength of spirit.
> Never set the law above these qualities,
> for they are meant to be limitless.

Rutilated Quartz—characterized by the presence of "needles" or strands of rutile (a titanium dioxide mineral) within the structure of the quartz crystal, it is thought to be highly energizing, bringing passion into difficult times or difficult projects. Some stones include golden rutile strands: a shimmering flicker of hidden treasure within, reminding us not only of the value of our own inner potential, but also the value that comes with it.

Job 28:9-12 VOICE: The miner breaks apart flinty stone, uprooting the ancient mountains. He carves tunnels through the rock, revealing precious treasures. He dams up the underground streams until they cease seeping, and he brings out into the light what was hidden there in the darkness. So where is wisdom found, and where does understanding dwell?

Smoky Quartz—unlike clear quartz, which is entirely translucent, smoky quartz has a dark, smoky color ranging from translucent grey to brownish-grey to black. Mirroring its smoky hue is smoky quartz's spiritual meaning, which represents grounding while letting go and surrendering old wounds.

Proverbs 15:30-33 TPT: Eyes that focus on what is beautiful bring joy to the heart, and hearing a good report refreshes and strengthens the inner being. Accepting constructive criticism opens your heart to the path of life, making you right at home among the wise. Refusing constructive criticism shows you have no interest in improving your life, for revelation-insight only comes as you accept correction and the wisdom that it brings. The source of revelation-knowledge is found as you fall down in surrender before the Lord. Don't expect to see Shekinah glory until the Lord sees your sincere humility.

Strawberry Quartz—symbolizes love for all, as well as love for self. Also symbolic of the destiny you were created for and the path you were always meant to take, and it is said to help you take the first steps on that path.

> Psalm 16:5-11 MSG: My choice is you, God, first and only.
> And now I find I'm your choice!
> You set me up with a house and yard.
> And then you made me your heir!
> The wise counsel
> God gives when I'm awake
> is confirmed by my sleeping heart.
> Day and night I'll stick with God;
> I've got a good thing going and I'm not letting go.
> I'm happy from the inside out,
> and from the outside in, I'm firmly formed.
> You canceled my ticket to hell—
> that's not my destination!
> Now you've got my feet on the life path,
> all radiant from the shining of your face.
> Ever since you took my hand,
> I'm on the right way.

River Stone

Known as the "Bones of Mother Earth," river stone is one of the oldest continually used stones for strength and energy. Culled from rivers and other moving bodies of water all over the world, river stone embodies the fluidity, vitality, movement, and purifying properties of water.

> Psalm 98:7-9 NLT: Let the sea and everything in it
> shout his praise!
> Let the earth and all living things join in.
> Let the rivers clap their hands in glee!
> Let the hills sing out their songs of joy before the Lord,
> for he is coming to judge the earth.
> He will judge the world with justice
> and the nations with fairness.

Rhyolite

Rhyolite is often called "Rain Forest Jasper," although it is, in fact, not a jasper at all. It symbolizes creativity and joy. Creativity is the language of the soul, and if you're listening, it might tell you to take a chance, especially if you're drawn to rhyolite. Rhyolite is said to have a radiant energy that infuses your spirit with pure joy, like an antidepressant but without any side effects.

Psalm 34:5 NLT: Those who look to him for help will be radiant with joy; no shadow of shame will darken their faces.

Ruby

Ruby is the deep red form of aluminum oxide (or corundum). While all other corundum gems along the color spectrum are given the name sapphire, the dark fiery red gives this gem its own unique classification as a ruby. Fine quality red rubies are very rare, which leads to their higher cost carat-for-carat than diamonds. Rubies were highly valued among the ancients too. According to *Gem and Minerals of the Bible*, "It was believed that the stone imprisoned a glowing spark, struck from the planet Mars, which would not dim or quench until the again earth itself grew sere and cold" (106). This fiery, glowing spark leads to its symbolism of vitality, energy, protection, and fierce courage. It is said to help one face controversy with strength to not back down.

Revelation 4:2-3 NIV: At once I was in the Spirit, and there before me was a throne in heaven with someone sitting on it. And the one who sat there had the appearance of jasper and ruby. A rainbow that shone like an emerald encircled the throne.

Sapphire

A pure variety of corundum (aluminum oxide) that is generally blue in color but can range from black to pink! Although used in various Bible translations, this gem was most likely not known or used until New Testament times (and/or it may have been referred to as hyacinth or jacinth instead—see scripture below). Any use of the word sapphire in the Old Testament most likely referred to lapis lazuli.

In the Orient, it was believed that Earth rested on a large sapphire and the sky was a bowl that reflected back the beautiful radiance of the blue gem. It was thought to attract divine favor. It is symbolic of heavenly wisdom and serenity, calming the mind, releasing depression, and alleviating spiritual confusion.

Revelation 9:17 AMP: And this is how I saw the horses and their riders in my vision: the riders had breastplates [the color] of fire and of hyacinth (sapphire blue) and of brimstone (yellow); and the heads of the horses looked like the heads of lions; and from out of their mouths came fire and smoke and brimstone (burning sulfur).

Sardonyx

A stone of strength and protection, sardonyx is a combination of sard (deep-red chalcedony) and onyx. As the stone is a combination of two stones, it brings the symbolism of both: sard/chalcedony symbolizes brotherly goodwill and peace-keeping, and onyx symbolizes memory. Together, with the fiery red of sard, it stands for deep commitment to those we love. In ancient times it was highly valued and often used for carvings and signet rings. A large number of cameos carved from sardonyx are in the Vatican Museum.

> Song of Solomon 8:6-7 AMP: Put me like a seal on your heart, like a seal on your arm; For love is as strong as death, Jealousy is as severe and cruel as Sheol (the place of the dead). Its flashes are flashes of fire,

[A most vehement flame] the very flame of the Lord!
Many waters cannot quench love, Nor can rivers drown it.
If a man would offer all the riches of his house for love,
It would be utterly scorned and despised.

Selenite

The "Stone of Purification," this soft, white crystal is a form of calcium sulfate (gypsum) with a beautiful, pearlescent luster. Dissolvable in water, it hints at its origins, as it is found where oceans once existed. Its name is derived from the Greek goddess of the moon, Selene, who lit up the night with her gentle, cascading light. Due to its "angelic" appearance, it has long been considered a spiritual stone. It symbolizes deep spirituality, purity, cleansing, gentleness, clarity, spiritual vision, and deep peace. It is extremely soft and can be scratched with your fingernail. It is said to help with the alignment and flexibility of the spine.

Genesis 16:7-13 NLT: The angel of the Lord found Hagar beside a spring of water in the wilderness, along the road to Shur. The angel said to her, "Hagar, Sarai's servant, where have you come from, and where are you going?"

"I'm running away from my mistress, Sarai," she replied.

The angel of the Lord said to her, "Return to your mistress, and submit to her authority." Then he added, "I will give you more descendants than you can count."

And the angel also said, "You are now pregnant and will give birth to a son. You are to name him Ishmael (which means 'God hears'), for the Lord has heard your cry of distress...

Thereafter, Hagar used another name to refer to the Lord, who had spoken to her. She said, "You are the God who sees me." She also said, "Have I truly seen the One who sees me?"

Serpentine

Because its mottled golden-green and grey color resembles snakeskin, giving it its name and meaning, serpentine symbolizes the powerful regenerative energy of this prehistoric reptile, a transformation of rebirth that's reflected in the snake shedding its skin. The ancients were often in awe of the snake and its legendary symbolism. Hermes, the father of alchemy, used the symbol of two intertwining snakes around a sword to represent healing.

Titus 3:4-6 VOICE: God our Savior and His overpowering love and kindness for humankind entered our world; He came to save us. It's not that we earned it by doing good works or righteous deeds; He came because He is merciful. He brought us out of our old ways of living to a new beginning through the washing of regeneration; and He made us completely new through the Holy Spirit, who was poured out in abundance through Jesus the Anointed, our Savior.

Sodalite

Named for its sodium content, blue sodalite symbolizes creativity, inspiration, focus, and clear communication, and has also been called the "Poet's Stone," the "Stone of Creatives," as well as the "Stone of Truth." Queen Victoria's granddaughter, Princess Patricia, was so inspired by the stone, she chose it for the interior decorations of Marlborough House in England. This prompted the stone's alternative name: "Princess Blue." So many names for this beauty!

Ephesians 2:10 AMP: For we are His workmanship [His own master work, a work of art], created in Christ Jesus [reborn from above—spiritually transformed, renewed, ready to be used] for good works, which God prepared [for us] beforehand [taking paths which He set], so that we would walk in them [living the good life which He prearranged and made ready for us].

Sunset Dumortierite

This aluminum boro-silicate mineral is named for the French paleontologist Eugene Dumortier who discovered it in the French Alps. It is believed to bring the wearer the energy of water: promoting flow, control, and orderliness.

> Proverbs 18:4 NLT: Wise words are like deep waters; wisdom flows from the wise like a bubbling brook.

Sunstone

Sunstone is a type of feldspar that, when viewed from certain directions, exhibits a sparkling appearance. Symbolizes joy, empowerment, vitality, wise leadership, and heightened intuition, and represents the true self joyfully and happily shining through. Said to dissipate fearfulness and alleviate stress, while encouraging independence, creativity, and originality. Especially helpful to those who have difficulty saying "No" to others.

Ephesians 2:4-10 VOICE: But God, with the unfathomable richness of His love and mercy focused on us, united us with the Anointed One and infused our lifeless souls with life — even though we were buried under mountains of sin — and saved us by His grace. He raised us up with Him and seated us in the heavenly realms with our beloved Jesus the Anointed, the Liberating King. He did this for a reason: so that for all eternity we will stand as a living testimony to the incredible riches of His grace and kindness that He freely gives to us by uniting us with Jesus the Anointed. For it's by God's grace that you have been saved. You receive it through faith. It was not our plan or our effort. It is God's gift, pure and simple. You didn't earn it, not one of us did, so don't go around bragging that you must have done something amazing. For we are the product of His hand, heaven's poetry etched on lives, created in the Anointed, Jesus, to accomplish the good works God arranged long ago.

Tiger's Eye

Tiger's Eye is a powerful stone symbolizing the release of fear and anxiety; increased harmony and balance; and the strength and courage to take action. It is said to help you to make decisions with discernment and understanding, unclouded by emotion.

> Proverbs 1:5 & 7 AMP: The wise will hear
> and increase their learning,
> and the person of understanding will acquire wise
> counsel and the skill [to steer his course wisely
> and lead others to the truth].
> …The [reverent] fear of the Lord [that is, worshiping Him
> and regarding Him as truly awesome]
> is the beginning and the preeminent part of knowledge
> [its starting point and its essence];
> but arrogant fools despise [skillful and godly] wisdom
> and instruction and self-discipline.

Blue Tiger's Eye—also called Hawk's Eye, it is a very soothing stone that is said to aid in reducing stress, increasing calm, and easing anxiety. Shimmery blue tiger's eye symbolizes the illumination of issues that may have been difficult to see otherwise, helping one speak with clarity and act from a place of integrity.

> Psalm 11:4 TPT: Yet Yahweh is never shaken
> —he is still found in his temple of holiness,
> reigning as King Yahweh over all.
> He is closely watches and examines
> everything man does.
> And with a glance, his eyes examine every heart,
> for his heavenly rule will prevail over all.

Topaz

A mineral consisting of aluminum, fluorine, oxygen, and silicon with superior hardness, topaz comes in a variety of colors including blue and golden-yellow. The name and meaning comes from the island named Topazios. According to ancient lore, *topazios* means to seek and apparently due to the island being shrouded by a dense layer of fog, mariners spent a great deal of time searching for the hidden island and its golden, glowing gems. Few gems can create static electricity, but interestingly, topaz can! Both a soothing and vibrant stone, it is symbolic of love, forgiveness, and friendship and is believed to bring beauty, intelligence, and a long life. On display at the National Museum of Natural History in Washington DC is a nearly 23,000 carat cushion-cut golden yellow topaz—for reference, that's the size of an automobile headlight!

Ecclesiastes 4:9-12 NIV: Two are better than one, because they have a good return for their labor: If either of them falls down, one can help the other up. But pity anyone who falls and has no one to help them up. Also, if two lie down together, they will keep warm. But how can one keep warm alone? Though one may be overpowered, two can defend themselves. A cord of three strands is not quickly broken.

Tourmaline

Classified as a semiprecious stone and occurring in a vast array of colors, its name it derived from the Sinhalese word *turamali*, which translates to "stone of many colors." Due to this variety of colors, tourmaline has often been confused with other stones, including rubies. It is said to be a stabilizing stone of reconciliation and receptivity, fostering compassion and attracting healing and friendship. It is also thought to be grounding, soothing, and calming, encouraging spirituality, wisdom, and meditation.

2 Corinthians 5:17-20 NLT: Anyone who belongs to Christ has become a new person. The old life is gone; a new life has begun! And all of this is a gift from God, who brought us back to himself through Christ. And God has given us this task of reconciling people to him. For God was in Christ, reconciling the world to himself, no longer counting people's sins against them. And he gave us this wonderful message of reconciliation. So we are Christ's ambassadors; God is making his appeal through us. We speak for Christ when we plead, "Come back to God!"

Turquoise

Turquoise symbolizes balance, truth, power, wisdom, luck, protection, and immortality. Prehistoric Native Americans used turquoise to symbolize "the god of the sky alive in the earth." There are many different types of turquoise, in a range of colors with a variety of names.

> Isaiah 42:5-7 NIV: This is what God the Lord says—
> the Creator of the heavens, who stretches them out,
> who spreads out the earth with all that springs from it,
> who gives breath to its people,
> and life to those who walk on it:
> "I, the Lord, have called you in righteousness;
> I will take hold of your hand.
> I will keep you and will make you
> to be a covenant for the people and a light for the Gentiles,
> to open eyes that are blind, to free captives from prison
> and to release from the dungeon those who sit in darkness."

Yellow Turquoise—although it comes from the same mines as turquoise, it is actually a serpentine stone with veins of hematite and/or quartz. Symbolic of communication, creativity, intuition, protection, and positive energy. With its warm and earthy colors, it connects the vibration of heaven with the energy of the earth.

Psalm 36:5 TPT: But you, O Lord, your mercy-seat love is limitless, reaching higher than the highest heavens. Your great faithfulness is infinite, stretching over the whole earth. Your righteousness is unmovable, just like the mighty mountains. Your judgments are as full of wisdom as the oceans are full of water. Your tender care and kindness leave no one forgotten.

Unakite

Unakite brings together the abundant, nurturing energy of green with the soft, caring passion of pink. Said to resonate with the frequency of love, it symbolizes compassion, kindness and emotional balance.

> Exodus 34:6 NLT: The Lord passed in front of Moses, calling out, "Yahweh! The Lord!
> The God of compassion and mercy! I am slow to anger and filled with unfailing love and faithfulness.
> I lavish unfailing love to a thousand generations."

Wonderstone

Wonderstone is a jasper with wave-like bands of charcoal gray, tan, cream, and mahogany brown. Flat, smooth stones are often used as worry stones, but instead of worry, a Wonderstone encourages us to enter a place of WONDER instead of worry and AWE instead of anxiousness.

> Psalm 33:6-8 VOICE: The unfathomable cosmos came into being at the word of the Eternal's imagination,
> a solitary voice in endless darkness.
> The breath of His mouth whispered the sea of stars into existence.
> He gathers every drop of every ocean as in a jar,
> securing the ocean depths as His watery treasure.
> Let all people stand in awe of the Eternal;
> let every man, woman, and child live in wonder of Him.

Wood Opalite

Wood opalite is a type of petrified wood that has been impregnated with the silicon dioxide commonly known as opal. Petrified wood is created through a process called permineralization, which takes millions of years. When wood becomes covered with earth, decays and is exposed to mineral-rich water, mineral deposits can create stone in the place of the decaying wood. Through this process, all organic parts are replaced by minerals, while retaining the structure of the wood. It is symbolic of the re-energizing power of the earth to bring life from places that are seemingly dead.

> Isaiah 60:16b-18 NLT: You will know at last that I, the Lord,
> am your Savior and your Redeemer,
> the Mighty One of Israel.
> I will exchange your bronze for gold,
> your iron for silver,
> your wood for bronze,
> and your stones for iron.
> I will make peace your leader and righteousness your ruler.
> Violence will disappear from your land;
> the desolation and destruction of war will end.
> Salvation will surround you like city walls,
> and praise will be on the lips of all who enter there.

Praying With Prayer Beads

With my love for rocks, I have found that I enjoy creating and praying with contemplative prayer beads. Prayer beads or prayer ropes are used across many spiritual traditions to help one focus in meditation and prayer. Traditional malas are used by Hindus and contain 108 beads. Rosaries are used within the Catholic tradition and often contain 50 beads. Chotki are used within the Orthodox Christian tradition and contain 33, 50, 100, 150 or more prayer beads (or knots instead of beads). Anglican prayer beads number 28 with four sets of seven, and the four beads used to separate the sets are called "Cruciform" beads as they form a cross.

Prayer beads, ropes and rosaries have traditionally been used to keep track of the number of prayers prayed. However, over time, the usage has changed from less repetition to more meditation and reflection. For folks who might struggle to stay still in prayer and meditation, the beads can provide a way to stay focused and attentive.

After I purchased my first mala, I began to research prayer beads and ropes from other religious traditions and eventually tore my mala apart to reconstruct it with more Christian symbolism. I call this Christ-centered version of prayer beads *Selah prayer beads*. The word *Selah* is taken from the Book of Psalms. Hebrew scholars believe it is a musical term indicating a place of pause, reflection or a place to take a breath. Selah prayer necklaces are constructed with 100 beads and the bracelet-sized version is created with 23. Other Christian prayer bead artisans will often create based on numbers that are significant to them within their own Christian tradition.

Most prayer beads have a tassel, and generally this is where you start your prayer. The tassel has a variety of meanings across traditions: most commonly, the kingdom of heaven, unity (the different strands are united together as one just as the body of Christ comes together as one), and also to be used to wipe the tears cried in contrition of sins.

Above the tassel is a pendant, cross or "guru" bead. I call this the "Jesus bead." As Christians we profess Jesus as our One True "guru" — our Rabbi and Teacher. As I hold the tassel and Jesus bead in the palm of my hand, I like to think of the body of Christ (represented by all the strands of the tassel) united under the Lordship of Jesus Christ, our Head.

From the Jesus bead, the necklace then branches out into two strands to make an unending circle to remind us to pray without ceasing (1 Thess 5:16).

As you pray, I suggest one of two things. First, you can simply hold the beads. The weight of the beads often feels grounding, and I enjoy feeling the cold stones warm to my touch as I hold them. If I get distracted, I use the tactile feel of twirling a bead between my fingers to bring my focus back to the present moment. A second way to pray is to work through the beads one-by-one to circle around the necklace or bracelet as many times as desired. I've included some directions below for this method.

Many Christ-centered prayer beads are constructed with number patterns of three, seven, ten and twelve or thirteen. Each number is significant in meaning:

- Three is symbolic of the Trinity.
- Seven is considered a holy number in both Jewish and Christian culture (Gen 2:2-3) and is the number of completeness.
- Ten is the sum of three and seven and symbolizes union and connection.
- Twelve symbolizes perfection or authority and represents the fullness of Jesus' kingdom and his reign and rule on earth as it is in. Some also like to use 13 to represent "12 disciples plus me."

Praying Through Your Prayer Beads:

Prayer beads may or may not follow the patterns indicated below so you will have to adjust the numbering sequences as needed.

Start by holding the tassel and Jesus bead in the palm of one hand, praying: **"United together under the Lordship of Jesus I pray in the name of the…"** (If the beads do not have a tassel and instead use only a focal bead, pray: **"Lord Jesus Christ, Center and Focus of my life I pray in the name of the…"**.)

Move to the 1st set of beads which is often three in number and pray: **"…Father, Son, Holy Spirit,"** acknowledging each member of the Holy Trinity.

At this point there is generally some kind of single bead or spacer bead that separates the first set of beads from the next. In my own design, I call this the Selah bead and use this as a place to pause, reflect and breathe. You'll often see these used to break up beads into groupings of three, seven, etc. No matter the grouping, I always use these as a place to pause, reflect and breathe. From there the necklace may continue with intervals of three, seven, ten, twelve (or thirteen). Below are a variety of prayers that are helpful for the various numbers of beads.

At some point you might find a grouping of beads around the back of the neck of no particular symbolic number. I generally use the first half of those beads to **"count my blessings"** and the second to offer prayers of gratitude for **intercession** to pray for family, friends and others in need. You can also pray for our world, our country, our communities, your neighborhood, and our leaders.

Prayers for Sets of Three (3):

- The Jesus Prayer (Luke 18:13):
  **Lord Jesus Christ,
  have mercy on me,
  a sinner.**

- St. Teresa of Avila:
    **Lord, you are
    closer to me than my own breath,
    nearer to me than my hands and feet.**

- St. Bridget:
    **Help me
    to love Jesus' gospel
    more fully.**

- Luke 17:28:
    **In him we live
    and move
    and have our being.**

- St. John of the Cross:
    **O Blessed Jesus, give me stillness of soul in You.
    Let Your mighty calmness reign in me.
    Rule me, O King of Gentleness, King of Peace.**

Prayers for Sets of Seven (7):

- The Lord's Prayer
- Colossians 1:15-20 (considered to be a hymn of praise)
- The Suscipe Prayer of St. Ignatius: **Take, Lord, and receive all my liberty, my memory, my understanding, and my entire will. All I have and call my own. You have given all to me. To you, Lord, I return it. Everything is yours; do with it what you will. Give me only your love and your grace, that is enough for me.**
- Sarah Coleman: **Father, today I ask forgiveness of all the negative and harmful words I have spoken about myself. I do not want to abuse myself in such a way again. Transform my thoughts and let me understand how marvelously you made me. Change my habits so I use my tongue to speak hope and favor upon my life.**

- Rick Warren: **Lord, I want to lay before you all that weighs heavy on my heart. Reveal even the sin I am not aware of, Lord. I lay these at your feet and pray your forgiveness on me. I believe you when you say that you wash us whiter than snow. Thank you Lord for your unending love for me! Help me start fresh right now to make choices that honor you. In Jesus' Name.**

- St. Teresa of Avila:
  **Let nothing disturb you,
  let nothing frighten you,
  all things will pass away.
  God never changes;
  patience obtains all things,
  whoever has God lacks nothing.
  God alone suffices.**

- St. Teresa of Avila:
  I am yours, you made me. I am yours, you called me. I am yours, you saved me. I am yours, you loved me. I will never leave your presence.

- St. Francis:
  May the Lord bless you. May He preserve you and turn His Face towards you. May He have mercy on you and give you his peace. May He show you always His Divine Glory and give you His Holy Approval.

- St. Anselm: **O Lord my God. Teach my heart this day, where and how to find you. Let me seek you in my desire; let me desire you in my seeking. Let me find you by loving you; let me love you when I find you.**

- St. Augustine Prayer for the Holy Spirit:
  Breathe in me O Holy Spirit, that my thoughts may all be holy. Act in me O Holy Spirit, that my work, too, may be holy. Draw my heart O Holy Spirit, that I love but what is holy. Strengthen me O Holy Spirit, to defend all that is holy. Guard me, then, O Holy Spirit, that I always may be holy.

- St. Augustine Prayer for the Sick:
  Watch O Lord, with those who cannot sleep or weep tonight. Tend your sick ones. Rest your weary ones. Bless your dying ones. Soothe your suffering ones. Pity your afflicted ones. Shield your joyous ones.

- St. Benedict: **Gracious and Holy Father, give us the wisdom to discover You, the intelligence to understand You, the diligence to seek after You, the patience to wait for You, eyes to behold You, a heart to meditate upon You, and a life to proclaim You, through the power of the Spirit of Jesus, our Lord.**

- Claire of Assisi: **Love enfolds. It is no longer I that live, but Christ that lives in me. I am secure in the Lord. I can look out, now, through the Lord's eyes. I can see the world as He created it, in His mercy, I can see my sisters and brothers with His love, and I can worship the Father through the eyes of the Son in the Love of the Holy Spirit.**

- St. Patrick: **Christ be with me, Christ within me,
  Christ behind me, Christ before me,
  Christ beside me, Christ to win me,
  Christ to comfort and restore me.
  Christ beneath me, Christ above me,
  Christ in quiet, Christ in danger,
  Christ in hearts of all that love me,
  Christ in mouth of friend and stranger.**

Prayers for Sets of Ten (10) beads: You can use or combine prayers from three and seven above or use these to beads to memorize or recite your favorite scripture verses. For example, St. Augustine's Prayer for the Holy Spirit above is easily broken down into ten even phrases.

Prayers for Sets of Twelve or Thirteen (12/13) beads:

- The Apostles Creed:
  I believe in God, the Father Almighty, maker of heaven and earth; And in Jesus Christ his only Son, our Lord; who was conceived by the Holy Spirit, born of the Virgin Mary, suffered under Pontius Pilate, was crucified, dead, and buried; descended into hell; the third day he rose from the dead; he ascended into heaven, and sits at the right hand of God the Father Almighty; and he will come to judge the living and the dead. I believe in the Holy Spirit, the holy catholic (or united) church, the communion of saints, the forgiveness of sins, the resurrection of the body, and the life everlasting. Amen.

- a time of silence

- I use this powerful prayer adapted and personalized from Ephesians 3:14-21:
  For this reason, I kneel before the Father, from whom every family in heaven and on earth derives its name. I pray that out of his glorious riches he may strengthen me with power through his Spirit in my inner being, so that Christ may dwell in my heart through faith. And I pray that I, being rooted and established in love, may have power, together with all the Lord's holy people, to grasp how wide and long and high and deep is the love of Christ, and to know this love that surpasses knowledge — that I may be filled to the measure of all the fullness of God. Now to him who is able to do

immeasurably more than all we ask or imagine, according to his power that is at work within us, to him be glory in the church and in Christ Jesus throughout all generations, for ever and ever! Amen.

The possibilities are endless here. There is no right or wrong way to pray through your beads. The only caution is not to allow your prayers to become meaningless and rout. Be creative. Use the beads in a way that is helpful to you in your own way of praying.

Where do I find my own prayer beads?

I have a few sources I'd like to refer to. These artisan friends are creating unique prayer beads with Christian symbolism. They use natural semi-precious stones like the ones listed in this book to fashion distinctive, one-of-a-kind creations. You won't find others wearing the same prayer beads as you. Working with intention and integrity, these artisans pray over the beads as they are designing, stringing and knotting.

Unique Peace by Amy:
www.amykuscsik.com/shop

Kristy DiGeronimo:
www.facebook.com/digeronimowellness

Good Vibrations by Kim:
www.facebook.com/goodvibrationsbykim

I also create a limited number of Selah prayer bead necklaces each year. You can reach out to me at yogafaithjody@gmail.com if you are interested in more information on that process.

The following section on color meanings might also prove helpful when choosing your own personal prayer beads.

Color Meanings

Colors can be a helpful clue to enhance the symbolism of your stones and gems. Here are typical meanings and scriptural references.

Red, Crimson, Scarlet — blood covering, blood of the Lamb, atonement, forgiveness, sacrifice, warfare, celebration, love of God. Exodus 26:14; Leviticus 17:11; Isaiah 1:18; Nahum 2:4; Hebrews 9:12-14; Revelation 6:3-4

Orange — praise, awe, consuming fire of God. Hebrews 12:29

Yellow, Amber — presence of God's glory, oil of gladness, celebration, joy. Psalm 68:13; Ezekiel 1:4 & 8:2; Isaiah 61:3; Hebrews 1:9

Green — healing, new beginnings, new life, refreshment, everlasting life, hope, growth, generosity, wealth, restoration. Psalms 23:2-3, 92:12-14; Proverbs 11:28; Jeremiah 17:8; Joel 2:22; Hosea 14:8; Mark 6:39; Revelation 22:2

Blue — grace, mercy, Holy Spirit, remembrance of God's deliverance and commands, heaven, living water, River of Life – Exodus 24:10-11; Numbers 15:38-41; Ezekiel 47:1-12; Revelation 22:1-2

Purple — royalty, kingship, honor, authority of believers, most precious of ancient dyes. Judges 8:26; Esther 8:15; Proverbs 31:22; Mark 15:17

Plum, Wine — richness, abundance, infilling of the Holy Spirit. Hosea 2:22; Joel 2:24

Pink — passion, rejoicing, joy, prophecy, also mix of red (love) and white (purity, innocence). 1 Samuel 18:6; Nehemiah 12:43

White — purity, innocence, holiness, light. Psalm 51:7; Is 1:18; Matthew 17:2; Revelation 3:4, 6:2, 7:9, 20:11

Black — righteous judgment, obedience to God's commandments, sin, death, famine, night. Exodus 10:15; Deuteronomy 4:11-13; Proverbs 7:9; Lamentations 4:8; Joel 2:10; Ephesians 5:8-11; Revelation 6:5

Brown, Gray, "Pale" — repentance, humility, death, destruction. Genesis 30:32-33; Esther 4:3; Daniel 9:3-5; Revelation 6:7-8

Silver — redemption, restitution, faith, truth, strength, refining. Genesis 20:16; Leviticus 5:15-16; Numbers 18:15-16; Psalms 12:6, 66:10, 68:13; Proverbs 25:4; Hosea 3:2; Matthew 26:14-15, 27:3-9

Gold, Amber — deity, divinity, glory of God. Exodus 37, 40:26-35; Psalms 21:3, 68:13; Hebrews 9:3-5; Revelation 1:12-16

Bronze, Brass — judgment, strength, perseverance (from refiner's fire), feet of God. Exodus 27, 30:17-21; Numbers 21:9; Ezekiel 40:3; Daniel 10:5-6; Micah 4:13; Revelation 1:15, 2:18

Orange, Yellow, White & Violet — this color combination is found in the hottest coals/flames of a fire. It represents God's Shekinah glory, purity, the invisible and supernatural, that which cannot be seen except with spiritual eyesight. Ezekiel 1:4, 8:2

White, Blue, Purple & Scarlet — this color combination is used throughout the tabernacle, temple, and on the priestly garments. It represents purity, remembrance, royalty, Divinity, God's Throne of Glory, and forgiveness. Exodus 25-28, 35-39; Isaiah 1:18

Rainbow — God's covenantal promise to all creation. Genesis 9:12-16

Iridescent — overcoming, New Jerusalem. Revelation 21:11

About the Author

Jody Thomae is the author of several books. All are available on Amazon.

- *God's Creative Gift – Unleashing the Artist in You*
- *The Creator's Healing Power – Restoring the Broken to Beautiful*

The interactive, in-depth devotional Bible studies listed above are part of the "Bible Studies to Nurture the Creative Spirit Within" series, written especially for those who enjoy artistry, beauty, creativity, and worship. Also available in Kindle.

- *Jesus In My Practice: Bringing the Questions of Jesus to My Movement, My Meditation & My Mat*
- *O My Soul: Bringing the Psalmist's Cry to My Movement, My Meditation & My Mat* (future release)

As the sub-titles suggest, these are geared towards creative, embodied spiritual practice. Includes journaling pages.

Jody also has a devotional album, *Song of the Beloved*, with original music and readings from scripture and Thomas à Kempis, available free through most musical outlets.

Her passion is for the revelation of Jesus to be made more real through creativity, embodied spirituality, and healing ministry. It is her desire to portray the message of Christ's desperate and unfailing love for his people to help sustain the hearts of the broken and weary. She is particularly interested in the reclamation of the body in the healing of traumatic and wounding events and works in the area of embodiment with those who have become disconnected from their bodies. She leads a series of retreats each year focused on Christian embodiment, creativity, and spirituality.

Additional Bible passage meditations, spiritual guidance, free creative resources, and inspiration can be found at jodythomae.com. Learn more about her retreat offerings at fullyembodied.com.

References

Gems and Minerals of the Bible by Ruth W. Wright and Robert L. Chadbourne, Harper & Row Publishers, 1970.

The Holy Scriptures

The Crystal Bible by Judy Hall. Penguin Publishing, 2003.

Made in the USA
Columbia, SC
08 January 2023